# Figure carving – the ethnic style
## Amazing world of possibilities

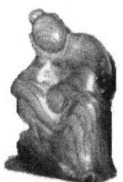

**By**
**Dr. King**
http://doctor-king-online.blogspot.com

# Also by Dr. King

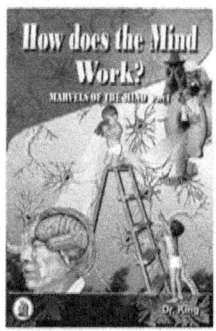
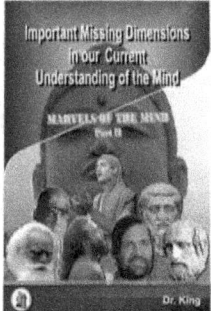
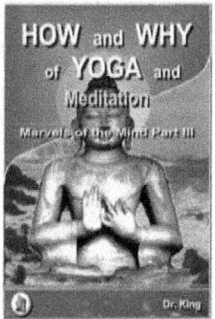
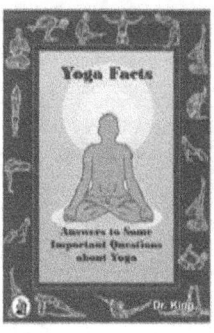
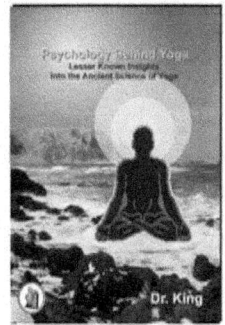
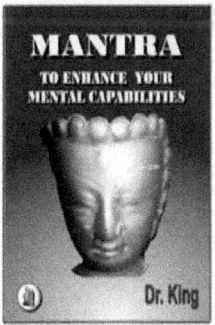
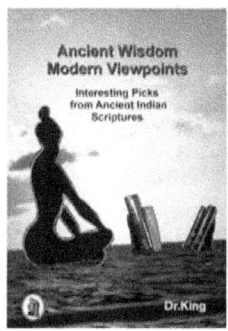
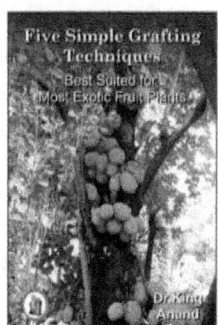
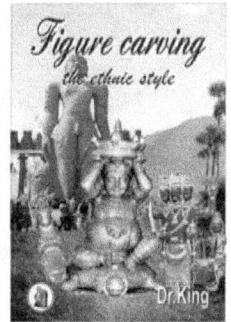

This book is available in three formats.

1.  Full colored e-book format
2.  Full colored paperback
3.  Grey colored 'economy edition' paperback

# Table of contents

Contact me at
          http://doctor-king-online.blogspot.com

# 1. In the carvers' village

**The** inspiration to write this book is my recent visit to a remote village that seemed to be a relic from a bygone era. In a way, it opened the doors to a magical world of figure carving. So it is only apt to begin this book with this memorable visit.

It was a small south Indian village well known for its carving tradition. Carvings made in this little village have gone all over the world and it hosts some of the world's largest monoliths. The village can better be called a big sculpture factory – almost every block has either a carver, or a carving school or a carving workshop! Wherever you look around, you can see a sculptor busy in action. The entire village is surrounded by black granite hills out of which most of the sculptures are carved. The village is rightly called 'the black stone' (*Karikal*) village.

As per the ancient Indian sculpture manuals – the 'Silpa Sästras' as they are called, figures carved out of black granite are the most suited for worship in temples. Though one sees mostly white marble figures in northern India, the south is black granite dominated. The particular variety of granite that is available in this village is relatively soft, fine grained and takes good mirror like polish. More than the Silpa Sästra, it is probably the easy availability of the stone and workability that have motivated the local carvers to select this stone.

## My meeting with a master sculptor

I first visited the house of a well known sculptor. He is second in the generation of sculptors, whose father had several master pieces to his credit. An almost 40ft tall - monolith carved under his guidance is installed in a nearby village. Another giant monolith of Buddha has been installed in Japan few years ago. Of course, given the size, the giant statue had to be sliced into manageable pieces, transported, and once again re-assembled in Japan.

Unlike in the west, carving in India is a family tradition running from generation to generation. There are particular castes that specialize in carving. The boys born in this caste are trained in carving right from their childhood. Actually, they are never formally trained; they just pick it up from their elders who carve for a livelihood. Or it may not be wrong to say that carving flows in their genes!

## Visit to a carving factory

I was led to the 'carving factory' attached to the house of the master sculptor. I am calling it a factory because the carving in these places is done almost like in an assembly line of an automobile factory! Carving is done stage by stage by different experts each specializing in a particular discipline.

First the master carver draws a rough sketch of the intended figure on the raw stone cut for the purpose. Next a sculptor who specializes in roughing works on it for several months depending on the size of the figure. He then passes it on to next guy who specializes in detailing. At this stage, different sculptors who specialize in different parts of the body would work on respective part – some on face, some on torso, and some on ornamentation and so on. After detailing, another set of specialists would rub and polish the figure. Finally, a coat of special oil based pigment is applied to the figure and the figure is ready for shipping!

Unfortunately, the day I visited this factory was a Sunday and there were very few carvers on duty. I met an old man – Kandasämi - who has been working for past 3 decades in this factory as a 'rough carver'. The poor fellow could speak and understand only his mother tongue which was Greek and Latin to me! But as they say, art has no language barriers and surprisingly after sometime, both of us were communicating with each other without much problem and I gathered lot of information about their tradition of sculpting.

Kandasämi told me that normally he spends two to three months on a figure of say 3ft tall – to chisel the stone into a rough resemblance of the final figure. When I asked him why he does not use modern electrical tools to cut and shape the stone and speedup the work, Kandasämi laughed and gestured to me that the modern tools are useless. They can, he said, never achieve the perfection that can be achieved using a simple chisel and a hammer.

It is not as if he did not have any electrical tools in the factory. In fact, he showed me several gadgets hung on the wall. But he said their use was limited. A simple homemade chisel, a hammer, a measuring device were all that he uses to carve the most marvelous figures in the world. The old Sanskrit adage rightly said 'perfection is achieved not by the tools but by the ability of the doer'!

The entire place was strewn with tens of figures each in different stage of carving. Some of them were even damaged and discarded. I kept wondering how a sculptor would have felt when a small mistake on his part or his fellow carver's part nullified his months of effort. Probably they don't care since carving is just their livelihood and not a passionate art! After all, they still get paid for what they sweated for.

I visited a carving school in the village too.

## The village carving school

When we approached the carving school I was greeted by the rhythmic sound of the wooden mallets cautiously tapping the chisels. I could see some boys sitting under the shades of trees and chatting together.

I was quite amazed at the grandeur of this residential school sprung up in a picturesque surrounding. Interestingly, the school is run by a Bank for charity purpose. It is setup for imparting training to poor village lads in different forms of carving. The school is open to anyone who would like to learn the art of carving. The students stay in this school for 18 months, learn whatever form of sculpture they would like, all for free. No fee is charged!. Once they finish their training, most of them find good placements.

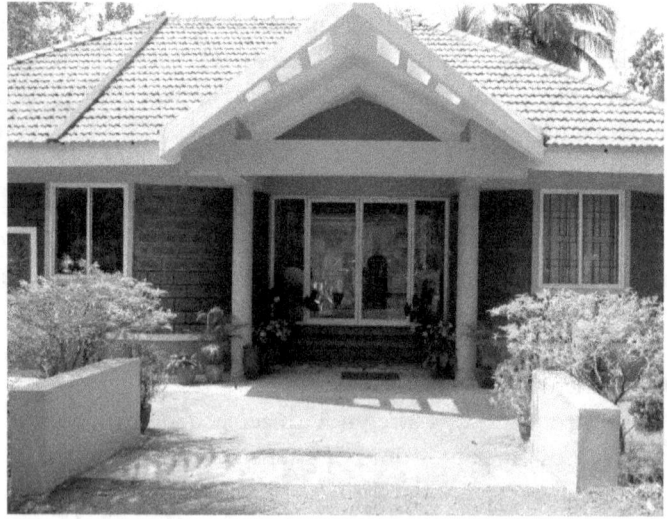

*Figure 1.1 The village carving school*

The school has separate departments for wood carving, stone carving, bronze casting, terracotta sculpting, embossing, and engraving, and so on. I could see some boys busy with their pet carving jobs even though it was a holiday.

What the students in this school are capable of doing is summarized by a 10 feet wide wooden panel, exquisitely carved, right at the entrance of the school. The panel depicted a royal court scene at the centre, flanked by royal caravan on either side of the centre piece.

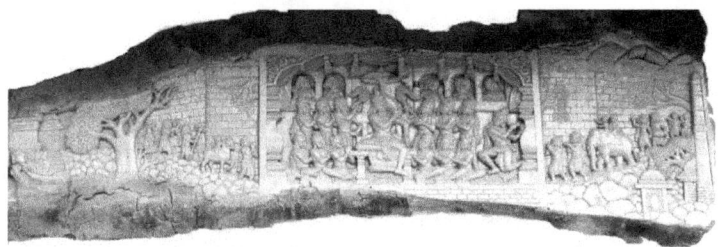

*Figure 1.2 A beautifully carved panel at the entrance of the school*

Most of the magnificent works of art created by these students were displayed all over the place. But unfortunately since it was a Sunday, we could see them only trough the locked glass doors, from a distance. There were stone statues, bronze castings as well as wooden figures, all beautifully carved.

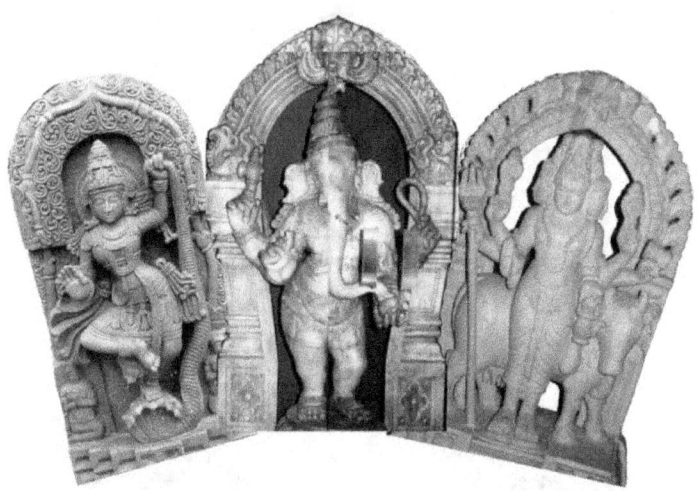

*Figure 1.3 Some sculptures carved by the students*

# My interest in carving

I learnt carving almost on my own and figure carving has always been my favorite. In fact, my very first carving was a figure of Buddha. Though I don't stick to any tradition or format, human figures somehow attract me as a subject for carving. For me carving is more of a form of meditation than art. And I love to completely get absorbed in carving for hours together.

One of my recent theme based carving done in the ethnic style is shown in Figure 1.4. It is my own composition that uses various hand gestures to drive home the message that one can be peaceful by respecting all (or surrendering to God), by not harming anyone, by not being over attached to worldly possessions and finally by regular practice of meditation. It is a 3ftX3ftX5inch relief.

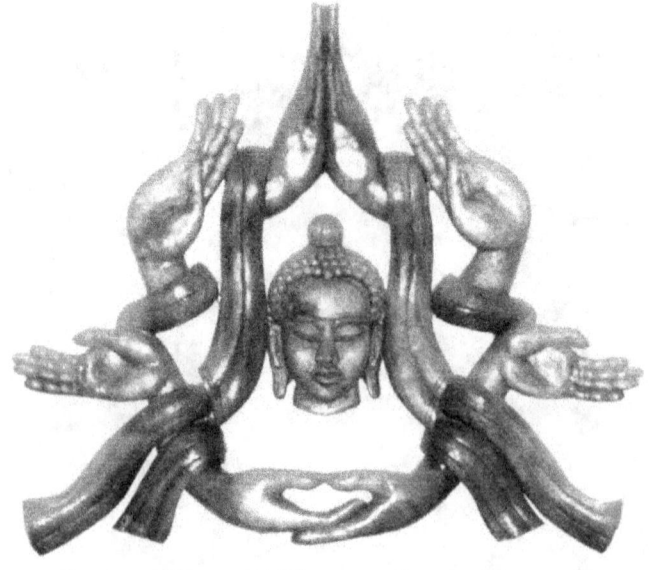

*Figure 1.4 The way to be peaceful*

Most people in the west carve as a hobby. The western tradition is to carve a figure precise to anatomical details and realism rules uppermost. As against this, the eastern carving tradition prevalent in India, south Asia and neighboring courtiers (I keep referring to this as the Indian subcontinent) has an altogether different emphasis. Here the anatomical precision takes the back seat. But more stringent rules of *Silpa Sästra* (sculpture manuals) take the upper hand.

A figure becomes perfect not because it is close to reality but because it adheres to the rules of the book to the very last fraction of an inch! Long back I had studied these ancient Silpa Sästra books just out of curiosity. But I never thought that these rules are followed even to this day. But they are, at least in southern India as I found when I visited this carving village.

In almost all the carving schools and factories that I visited in this small carvers' village, I kept hearing the one word – 'tälamäna'. Before the students are taught the actual carving techniques, they are first trained in 'tälamäna' for nearly a month. What is this tälamäna? That is what I will be talking about in the next chapter.

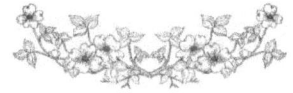

# 2. Carving to 'book precision'

**For** people who are used to western style of figure carving, it may look strange that someone carves by looking up measurements of different body parts from a book. We rarely do that, though we do have rough measures in terms of head sizes and the like. Most of the time, the figure carving is done by keeping a model (either human or clay) in front and implicitly mimicking the fine details of the model. Often the body measurements are done mentally, by careful visual observation.

As compared to this, the figure carving that I am going to talk about in this book relies more on precisely laid out body measurements which may or may not exactly correspond to reality. This was what was followed by all traditional carvers for thousands of years in countries spanning from Afghanistan to Cambodia, from Himalayas to far southern regions like Indonesia (see Chapter 6 for some excellent examples of these sculptures).

There was uniformity in tradition, faiths, social structure in all these regions, with today's India forming the heartland. And like all the ancient traditions and faiths, it is still alive and thriving in India, though what we see today may be in a far diluted state than what it was thousands of years ago.

This kind of 'carving to book precision' was important for the following reasons.

- Figure carving almost always had a religious connotation and the carved figures were seen as motifs of divinity. Only a precisely – as per the book – carved figure was acceptable for worship in the temples.

- The figures were not just restricted to human figures but also to a range of human like (in appearance) figures, be it the Gods and Goddesses, demons, spirits, angels, nymphs, imps and so on. So having a live model was ruled out.

- These figures were viewed more as aids to meditation rather than as works of art. A precisely carved image based on the measurements given in the book and following the details given in respective 'meditative verses' (*dhyāna shloka*) was supposed to evoke the necessary mood for meditation.

- Carving was more of a bread earner for many artisans rather than a hobby. Large scale 'production' of these sculptures employing thousands of artisans made it inevitable to have a book that precisely lays down each detail so that there is uniformity in the figures carved. The standardization is so unique that well trained eyes can immediately recognize an image carved as per the book!

- Giant monoliths –several tens of feet tall - that are common place in these regions could only be carved using the precise measurements given in a book. Mere eye estimates would not help in such cases.

This system of 'carving by the book' was supposed to have been followed in these regions for thousands of years. Several books called *Silpa Sästra*, describing these systems exist even to this day and are meticulously followed. To cite some of the typical Silpa Sästra books that are in vogue even to this day, there is the widely used Kasyapa Silpa Sästra, not so well known Manasara Silpa Sästra, Sakaladhikara, Maya Silpa, Brahmiya Citra Karma Sästra, Saraswatiya Citra Karma Sästra, and so on.

The Silpa Sästras laid out elaborate set of rules for carving various figures, both divine as well as human. Originally these rules were passed from generation to generation purely in an oral tradition. Even just a century ago, a sculpture student had to commit these rules to memory, orally transmitted to him by his teacher! But today, many of these appear in book form albeit having gone through several transformations in the process of shift from oral to written tradition.

## The Kasyapa Silpa Sästra

The specific system I discuss in this book is based on the ancient *Kasyapa Silpa Sästra* which is attributed to author Kasyapa. The exact date of composition of this book is uncertain but is believed to be sometime before 500 B.C. But this composition went through a series of transformations throughout the ages and the final form as it is available today may have been frozen in late $10^{th}$ or $11^{th}$ centuries.

There are other Silpa Sästras that are also used by sculptors in various parts of this region but Kasyapa Silpa Sästra seems to be the most popular and most comprehensive. This book is so elaborate that it may be impossible to cover it completely here. I will only try to pick some relevant details, focusing mainly on carving human figures. I will only do a cursory coverage of other figures.

As I said in the previous chapter, in common parlance the word used for this carving system is *tälamäna*. Different books may list out slightly different set of body measurements, but all of them are collectively called 'the tälamäna'. Let us look a bit more in detail about this tälamäna.

# Tälamäna – the precise system of body measurements

The word tälamäna is made up of two words – täla (palm) and mäna (measure) - which essentially means the measures of palms. Just like we have our imperial system of measurement where the length is measured in terms of feet, the tälamäna system uses the length of palms. The palm length is measured from the tip of the middle finger to the wrist joint or as the distance between the tip of the middle finger and that of the thumb when the palm is stretched out.

Just like the *foot* measure, the täla is also divided into 12 equal parts called *angula* (akin to *inch* in the imperial system). Each angula is further divided into 8 equal parts called *yava*. For notational convenience I will indicate angula by the symbol '^' and yava by '~'. For example, the length five angula two yava is indicated as 5^2~. However, not to be very pedantic, I often use decimal system and skip the yava notation.

But as we see later, this similarity between the *feet* measure and the *palm* measure is superficial. While the feet system talks about an absolute measure, the täla system on the other hand is a relative measure. We will discuss that later.

When we say figure carving, we normally mean carving human figures. But this region with its rich mythology and deep routed religious faith, figure caring is not just limited to human figures. Instead, most of the time it refers to carving one of the myriad varieties of human like figures corresponding to various beings that are human like in appearance.

## Categories of human like beings

Most religions in this region (and probably elsewhere in the world) believe in the existence of several beings that have a human like form. Since the primary purpose of carving figures is religious, figures of several human like beings are also traditionally carved.

The Kasyapa Silpa Sästra puts different kinds of beings into 10 major categories. The name of the category denotes the median height of a being (in terms of täla) in that category. For example, category 10 has beings whose median height is 10 täla units (*Dasa täla*). On the other hand, the shortest of the beings are put in category 1 (*Eka täla*) whose height is just 1 täla. While most major Gods fall in category 10, Imps and other miniature beings belong to category 1. In this range of beings, humans fall in category 8 (*Ashta täla*).

Each of these 10 major categories is further divided into 3 subcategories – upper (*Uttama*), middle (*Madhyama*) and lower (*Adhama*) subcategory. The upper subcategory is 1/3 täla taller than the middle sub category and the lower subcategory is 1/3 täla shorter than the middle sub category. In this way, there are altogether 30 categories in the tälamäna of Kasyapa Silpa Sästra.

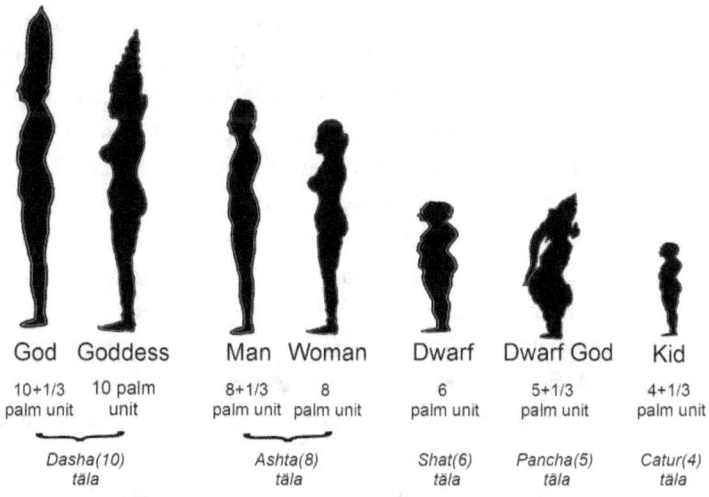

| God | Goddess | Man | Woman | Dwarf | Dwarf God | Kid |
|---|---|---|---|---|---|---|
| 10+1/3 palm unit | 10 palm unit | 8+1/3 palm unit | 8 palm unit | 6 palm unit | 5+1/3 palm unit | 4+1/3 palm unit |
| | Dasha(10) täla | | Ashta(8) täla | Shat(6) täla | Pancha(5) täla | Catur(4) täla |

*Figure 2.1 Some of the figure categories in the tälamäna system*

Though not uniform throughout, upper subcategories denote male members of that category. Similarly the middle subcategory is used for female figures and the lower subcategory for attendants or subordinates in the same category.

Accordingly human male figures belong to upper category 8 (*Uttama ashta täla*) and human females belong to middle category 8 *(Madhyama ashta täla)*. There is a category – category 6 – for dealing with figures that are dwarf with deformed features like hunch back etc.

Category 5 generally deals with Gods who are believed to be dwarfs or have a child like appearance – for example the elephant headed Ganesa or the monkey featured Hanuman. Similarly, category 4 deals with kids. Some of these categories are shown in Figure 2.1

## Täla as a relative measure

When I talked about *täla* earlier, I said it is like the *feet* in the imperial system of measurement. But this similarity is superficial. While the *feet measure* is based on the fixed length of an idealized foot, täla is a relative measure. Also, it is used more as a convenient word for nomenclature rather than as a word that corresponds to any physical palm length ideal or otherwise.

This relative definition of length of the täla as well as the angula makes it convenient to specify the body measurements relative to the height of the figure without the need to specify them for each instance of the figure in that category. All that the carver has to do is to compute the angula measure once for the intended figure and use that measure for all actual measurements. It is as if using different *foot rule* for different instances of figures.

The actual length of a täla depends on the physical height of the intended figure and the category to which the figure belongs. The way the length of a täla is calculated is as follows.

1. First decide the physical height of a figure (in conventional measurement).
2. See to which category the figure belongs.
3. See what the palm measure for that category is.
4. Now divide the height by the palm measure for the category.
5. The ratio thus calculated is the length of the täla for that figure.
6. This length divided by 12 gives the physical length of an angula for that figure.
7. Alternately you can use the total height of the figure in that category in terms of angula to compute the physical length of the angula directly.

For example, let us say we want to carve a female figure of height, say, 5 feet 4 inches. The necessary steps for the angula computation are as follows.

1. Total physical height of the figure is 5X12+4 (5ft 4 inches) = 64 inches.
2. The figure falls in category 8 (height in terms of täla).
3. So the length of the täla is (physical height)/( height in terms of täla )= 64/8 = 8 inches.
4. The physical length of an angula is 8/12 = 2/3 inch.

Alternately
1. Height of the figure in terms of angula = 96 (from the book).
2. The physical length of the angula is 64/96 = 2/3 inch.

I will take up a more detailed example of various computations in 3.

With this overview of the tälamäna system in general, let us get down to detailed measurements of various figures in the next chapters. I will focus mainly on measurements pertaining to human figures and as a special case of interest, those of dwarf Gods.

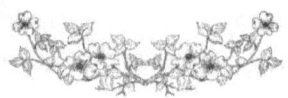

# 3. Carving human figures

**Given** the fact that there are as many as 30 categories of beings in the tälamäna system of Kasyapa Silpa Sästra, it is quite an elaborate set of measurements. Such details are definitely needed for someone who wants to carve varieties of figures. But they are too exhaustive and probably a bit monotonous for a casual reader.

In this book, I am not going to get into the detailed measurements for each of these categories. Instead, I will restrict myself to category 8 which deals with human figures. More specifically, I will discuss measurements of male figures – upper category 8 - as a typical example. There are 4 types of measurements.

1. Distance between two specific points/reference lines on the body.
2. Width of a particular part of the body at a specific place.
3. Length of a body part between two clearly demarcated points.
4. Girth of a specific body part

In a book with sketches, it may be easier to show these measurements as I have done in subsequent pages. But the silpa Sästra was originally passed orally without being recorded in a book form. So the measurements had to be descriptive rather than pictorial. So, these Sästras often assumed different well defined reference points or lines passing through these points as a basis for measurements that are verbally described. Even in books with visual sketches, it may be more precise to indicate these measurements with reference to these lines or points.

In this book however, I will almost always indicate the measurements pictorially rather than verbally for the sake of brevity. Let us first look at these reference point or lines.

# Various reference points/lines

The Silpa Sästra defines some specific points on the body of the figure and lines –horizontal or vertical – passing through these points. These lines are called the reference lines (*sootra*). These lines are defined both in the front view of the figure as well as in its side view.

Table 3-1 and Table 3-2 list various reference lines in the front view of the figure. The words given in the parenthesis are the traditional Sanskrit names of these reference lines.

*Table 3-1 Horizontal reference lines in the front view*

| | |
|---|---|
| **Top of head line** (*Ushneesha sootra*) | Horizontal line passing through the highest point on the head. |
| **Lower hair line** (*Kësänta sootra*) | Horizontal line touching the hair line on the forehead. |
| **Brow line** (*Bhroo sootra*) | Horizontal line touching the top of the eye brows. |
| **Eye line** (*Akshi sootra*) | Horizontal line touching the bottom of the eyes. |

| | |
|---|---|
| **Tip of nose line** (*Näsä putänta sootra*) | Horizontal line touching the tip of the nose. |
| **Chin line** *(Hanvanta sootra)* | Horizontal line touching the chin. |
| **Neck pit line** *(Hikkä sootra)* | Horizontal line passing through the pit below the neck. |
| **Breast line** *(Stana sootra)* | Horizontal line touching the bottom edge of the breasts. |
| **Navel line** *(Näbhi sootra)* | Horizontal line passing through the centre of the navel. |
| **Genital line** *(Mëdhra moola sootra)* | Horizontal line passing through the point where the genitals start. |
| **Thigh end line** (*Urdhvanta sootra*) | Horizontal line passing through the ends of the thighs |
| **Lower leg line** *(Jänu sootra)* | Horizontal line passing through the bottom edge of the knee joints. |
| **Ankle line** *(Nalikä sootra)* | Horizontal line passing through the ankle joints. |

| | |
|---|---|
| **Ground line** (Bhoomi sootra) | Horizontal line touching the ground below the feet. |

*Table 3-2 Vertical reference lines in the front view (one on either side of the centre line)*

| | |
|---|---|
| **Centre line** (*Madhya sootra*) | Vertical line passing through the middle of the body. |
| **Nostril line** (*Puta paryanta sootra*) | Vertical lines touching the edges of the nostrils. |
| **Face line** (*Mukha paryanta sootra*) | Vertical lines touching the outer edge of the face. |
| **Ear line** (*Karna sootra*) | Vertical lines touching the outer edges of the ears. |
| **Armpit line** (*Kaksha sootra*) | Vertical lines passing through the armpits |
| **Shoulder line** (*Bähu paryanta sootra*) | Vertical lines touching the outer edges of shoulders |

A three dimensional figure also has thickness in addition to height and breadth. To indicate the thickness at various point of the figure, the Silpa Sastra uses reference lines with respect to which the distances in the third dimension are given. Table

3-3 lists these reference lines.

*Table 3-3 Vertical reference lines in the side view*

| | |
|---|---|
| **Front line** (*Poorva sootra*) | This is a vertical line touching the tip of the nose, chest and the lower abdomen. |
| **Centre line** (Madhya sootra) | This is vertical line passing through the centre of the body. |
| **Back line** (Para sootra) | This is a vertical line touching the back. |

Figure 3.1 shows various reference lines – both horizontal as well as vertical – in the front view of the figure. In this figure, only single instance of each vertical reference line is shown for the sake of clarity. In reality there is a pair of lines on either side of the centre line.

Similarly Figure 3.2 shows various reference lines in the side view of the figure. These are used to indicate distances in the third dimension.

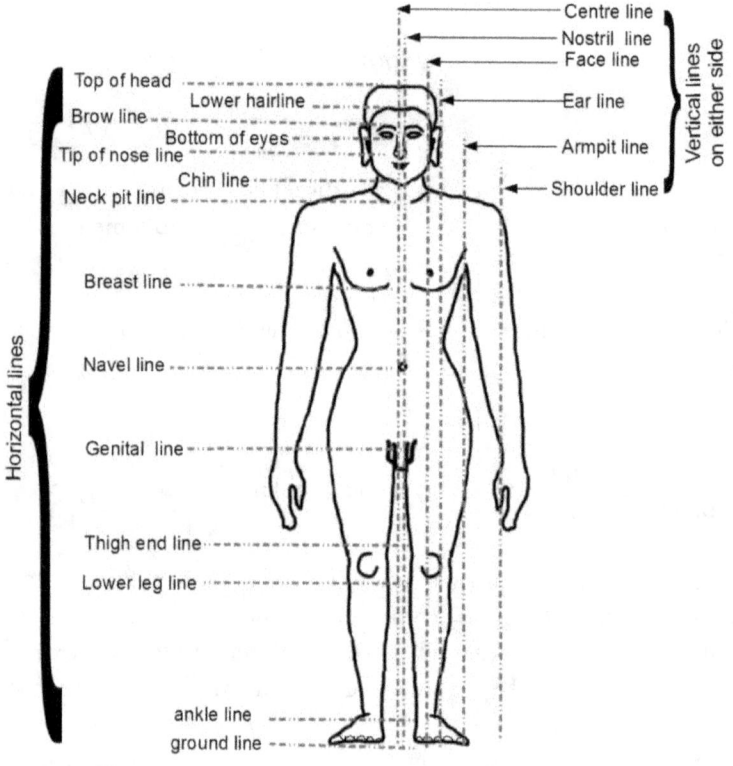

*Figure 3.1 Reference lines on the front view of a figure*

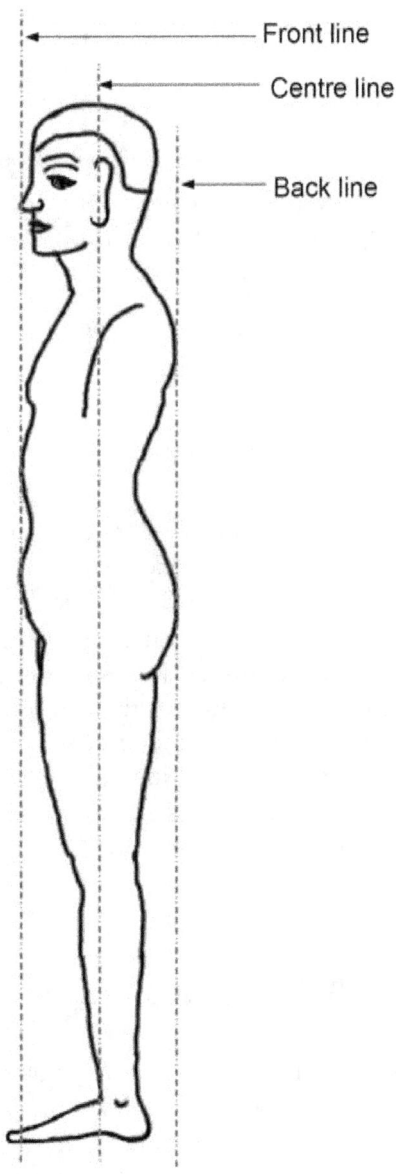

— Front line

— Centre line

— Back line

*Figure 3.2 Reference lines on the side view of the figure*

The Silpa Sästra uses these reference lines to verbally list out various body measurements. For example, the verbal description of various measurements for figures in category 10 goes as follows.

*"Let me now describe the measurements for upper category 10. Listen carefully. The total height of the figure – from the top of the head (Ushneesha) to the bottom of the foot - is "Veda + 20 +100" (Saveda Vimsadamsam ca satam ) i.e. 124. The top of the head (Ushneesha) is "Candra +3 yava" (triyavadhika Candramsa) i.e. 1^3~. From there to the lower hair line it is "Agni" i.e. 3^ ............ and so on (Kasyapa Silpa Sästra Chapter 55)*

A point to note is that the Silpa Sästra uses several mnemonics instead of numbers to denote measurements, for example, Veda for 4, Candra for 1, Agni for 3 and so on. Probably this was to make the description easy to remember. For anybody familiar with ancient Indian scriptures, the mnemonics are very clear. But in this book I use pictorial illustrations to provide a quick summary of various measurements instead of these verbose descriptions.

With these reference points/lines defined, let me next give the distances between these lines for male human figures. The details for other figures are similar and I skip them for brevity.

# Detailed body measurements

The details given in the Silpa Sästra are quite exhaustive. Reproducing all of them here is not only quite bulky but also a bit monotonous. What I intend to do is to show only some of the prominent measurements for the sake of brevity.

For ease of illustration, I will divide the body into three parts vertically and indicate some of the measurements given in the Sästra. The measurements are given in terms of *angula* indicated by '^'. Refer to Chapter 2 for the definition of *angula* and how it is calculated based on the total height of the figure and the category into which the figure falls.

## Head portion

Head portion is the most prominent portion of any figure and definitely more detailed measurements are needed. Some of these measurements in terms of *angula* are as shown in Figure 3.3. The dotted lines with reference to which the measurements are given are the reference lines we talked about in the previous section.

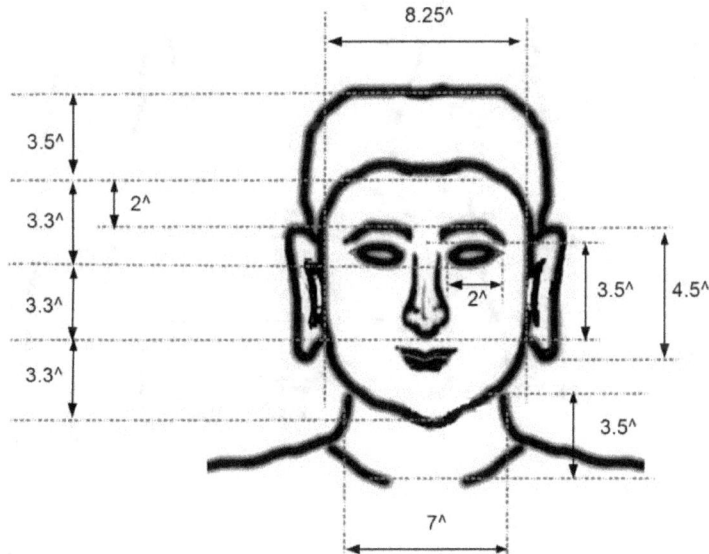

*Figure 3.3 Head measurements*

In some cases, the measurements are that of a specific part of the body; say for example, the width of the eye, or the length of the nose, and so on as shown in Figure 3.3. There are many more detailed measurements that are given in the Silpa Sästra that I have skipped here for brevity.

## Middle portion of the body

Next let me show the measurements corresponding to the middle part of the body. These measurements are as shown in Figure 3.4.

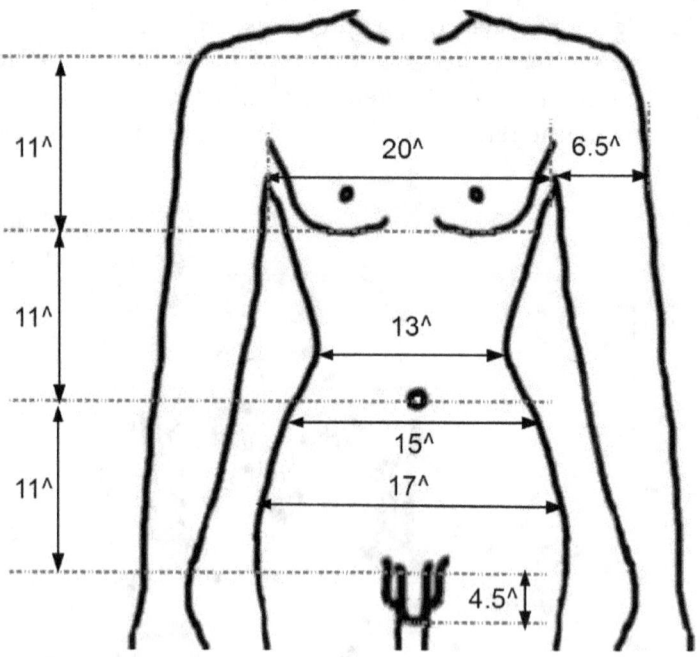

*Figure 3.4 Measurements corresponding to middle of the figure*

Even here, I have shown only some typical measurements and skipped the rest.

## Lower part of the body

Some of the measurements corresponding to the lower part of the body are as shown in Figure 3.5.

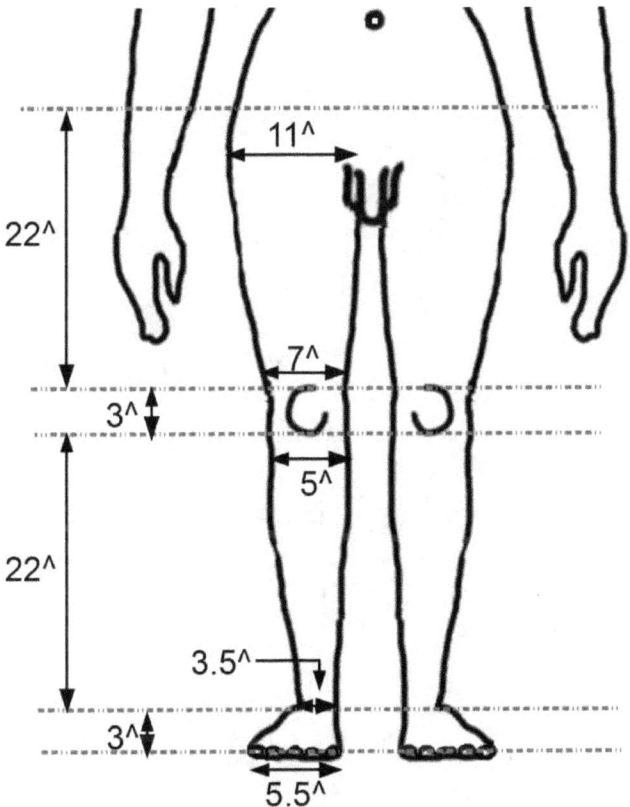

*Figure 3.5 Lower body measurements*

The book also specifies detailed measurements of different parts of the body in terms of their length, width and girth. For example, some of the measurements corresponding to the hand are as shown in Figure 3.6.

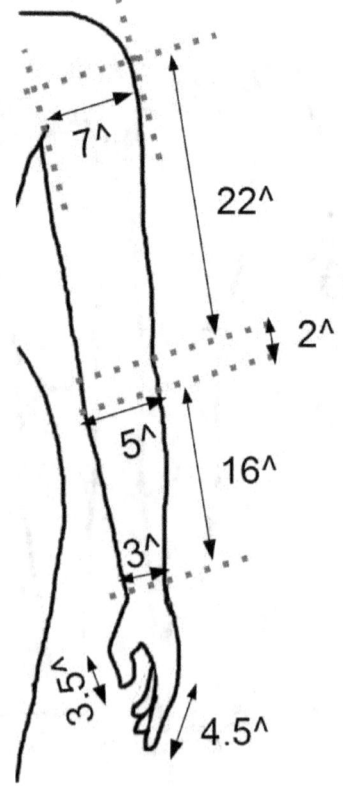

*Figure 3.6 Hand measurements*

Whatever I have listed in the previous sections are only measurements corresponding to the front view of the body. In a three dimensional figure, it is important to know not only the measurements corresponding to the front view of the figure but also to the side view of the figure such as the thickness of the chest for example. The book does give detailed measurements for the side view as well. Figure 3.7 shows some of these measurements.

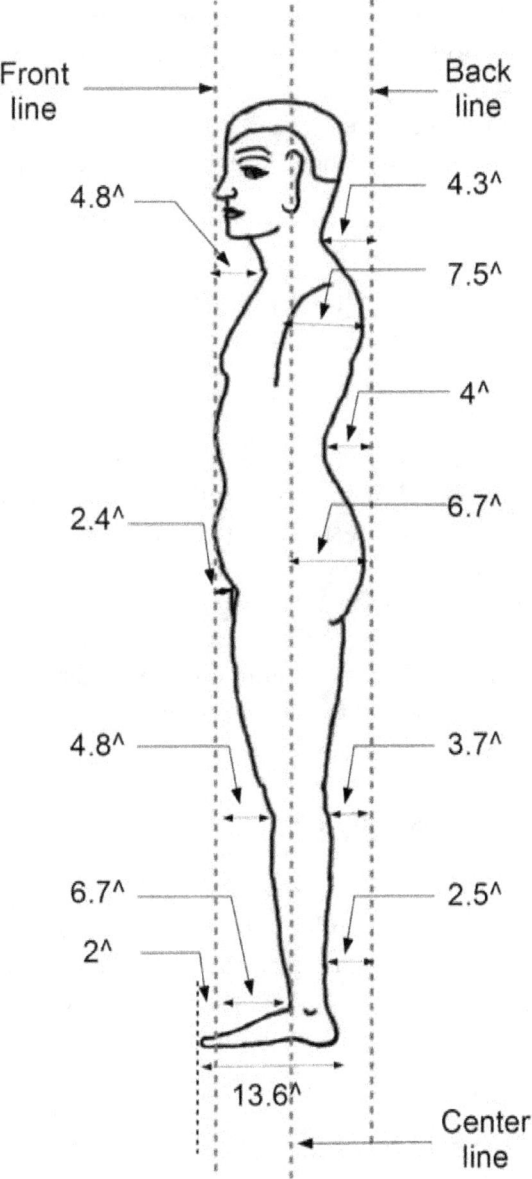

Front line

Back line

4.8^

4.3^

7.5^

4^

6.7^

2.4^

4.8^

3.7^

6.7^

2.5^

2^

13.6^

Center line

*Figure 3.7 Body measurements in the side view*

Please note that though I have given only the measurements

corresponding to male human body, similar set of measurements are also provided for the female human body by the Silpa Sästra. In both cases the Sästra leaves no part of the body uncovered – including genitals and other private parts.

Let me next illustrate further how these measurements are actually used in carving a figure suing a typical example.

# A simple illustration of carving a real figure

What I have discussed in the previous sections are the relative measurements of a human figure with reference to various reference lines. Now let us see how these measurements are used in practice. Let us say, we want to carve a figure like the nude male figure shown on the cover page.

This monolith is carved centuries ago using granite rock. The height of this figure is around 60 ft. excluding the pedestal. How does one go about carving a figure of this mammoth size? This involves at least the following steps.

## Compute the absolute measurements

Since the carving is done not by visual guidance, but by actually measuring the various body parts, one needs to first calculate absolute measurements using the relative measurements given in the Silpa Sastra that we discussed in the previous sections. This involves the following steps.

### Step 1: Compute the absolute length of the angula.

This figure is that of a king namely Bähubali who renounced his kingdom centuries ago and stood naked performing the

penance. I will come to historical details in Chapter 6. This figure falls in upper category 8 (human male figure). The total
height of a figure in upper category 8 as we saw earlier is 100
angulas.

Since the desired height of the figure we want to carve is 60
ft, the absolute angula length works out to 60/100 ft or 0.6ft or
7.2 inches.

## Step 2: Compute absolute lengths of various body parts.

To get these measurements all that you have to do is to multip-
ly various body measurements listed out in Figure 3.3, Figure
3.4, Figure 3.5, Figure 3.6, and Figure 3.7 by the absolute length
of an angula computed above.

For example, the width of the face (refer to Figure 3.3)
would be 8.25 X 7.2 = 59.4 inches or approximately 5 ft., the
height of the face would be 13.5 X 7.2 = 97.2 inches or approximately 8 ft. Similarly, the total length of the hand up to the
wrist (refer to Figure 3.6 ) would be 40 X 7.2 = 288 inches or
approximately 24 ft, and so on.

## Step 3: Compute the absolute thickness of the figure at various points.

Now refer to Figure 3.7 to compute the thickness of the figure
at various points. For example, the maximum thickness of the
figure would be $2^{\wedge}$ + 2 X $6.7^{\wedge}$ = 15.4 ^ (2 ^ foot extension
from the front line and 6.7 ^ on either side of the centre line at
the buttocks). In terms of absolute measures, this works out to
15.4 X 7.2 = 110.88 or approximately 9.25 ft. Other thickness
measurements are also computed accordingly.

## Compute the size of the rock slab needed

Normally, in addition to the visible part of the figure, a stub of suitable size is included at the bottom end of the figure if the figure is meant to stand alone. This stub is normally inserted into a hole in the ground or the pedestal, to make the figure stand upright without being unstable. Let us assume that the height of the stub below the figure is around 10 ft. This would make the total height of the figure 60+10 = 70 ft.

Now calculate the breadth of the figure. Refer to Figure 3.4 for this. The measurements that contribute to this breadth are the chest width, shoulder width, plus something extra to account for the maximum horizontal stretch of the arms. The last one is flexible and let us assume that it is one shoulder width on either side. The total works out to 20 ^ (chest) + 2 X 6.5^ (shoulders) + 2 X 6.5 ^ (shoulder spread on either side) = 46^. In terms of absolute measure, this works out to 46 X 7.2 = 331.2 inches or approximately 28 ft. This is the breadth of the figure.

Next compute the thickness of the figure. As we already calculated above, this thickness is around 9.25 ft.

To account for safety margins, we need to add some extra to each of these measurements. Let us say that we add 10% extra. That means we need a slab of roughly 77ft X 31ft X 11ft size to carve this figure.

We may also need to compute the rough weight of this stone slab. This may ne needed to plan the transportation mechanisms needed to move the slab from the quarry to the actual carving site, or the effort needed in erecting the figure.

Assuming the density of granite is around 100 Kg/ cubic feet, the total weight of this stone slab would be 77 X 31 X 11 X 100 /1000 = approximately 2600 tons! It is beyond imagination how a rock of this size and weight was moved centuries ago when this figure was actually carved!

## The process of carving

Assuming that the needed rock slab is actually separated from the mother rock and moved to the actual site, the first thing that is done by the master carver would be draw the rough sketch of the figure on the slab as shown in Figure 3.8.

First, various reference lines are drawn on the slab. The body measurements computed earlier would be used to draw this sketch since visual guidance is almost ruled out, given the colossal size of the figure.

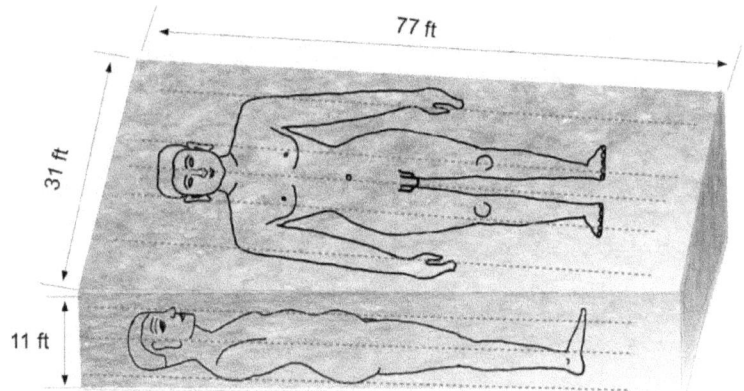

*Figure 3.8 Rough sketch of the figure drawn on the stone slab,*

Literally hundreds of skilled carvers work on various regions of the figure, each armed with precise pre-computed measurements of various body parts. This is where the precisely; listed out measurements come handy.

Well, the actual process is not as easy as it sounds since it involves coordinated efforts of hundred of carvers working together on the same figure and when the visual guidance is almost impossible.

What we discussed in this chapter are measurements related to normal adult male body. The Silpa Sästra is so meticulous that it also covers abnormal adult bodies such as hunch backs or dwarfs as well as normal kids who have slightly different body measurements as compared to adult bodies. Another interesting case is that of dwarf Gods who are very popular in Hindu mythology. I will discuss these things very briefly in the next chapter.

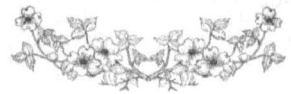

# 4. Carving figures of dwarfs, dwarf Gods and kids

The Kasyapa Silpa Sästra deals with each and every possible being, starting from Gods, humans, down to imps and miniature creatures. However the major emphasis has always been on carving divine figures. As we saw in the previous chapter, the Sästra deals in sufficiently great detail about normal adult human figures that fall in the category 8.

In real life, humans can be dwarf, or deformed with a bent or hunchback, or even be kids. Similarly, the Gods can be of normal height or they can even be dwarfs. In this chapter, I will briefly talk about these special cases of humans and Gods and how the Silpa Sästra handles them.

## Carving dwarf human figures

The Sästra deals with dwarf human figures in category 6. Though the details are quite sketchy, it does emphasize on the major differences between normal adult human figures and dwarf or deformed human figures. In particular, while the normal human figures are 8 1/3 palm length tall (for male figures), the corresponding dwarf figures are only 6 palm length tall. The comparison between the normal male figure and a dwarf male figure is summarized in Figure 4.1.

Following points of difference between normal adult male body and that of a dwarf can be noted in Figure 4.1.

1. Relativistically, while the normal adult male is 100 angula tall, the corresponding dwarf is only 72 angula tall.
2. The genital start line in normal adult male figure is exactly at the centre of the body (i.e. at 50 angula). Where as in the dwarf figure it is slightly higher (i.e. 40^ instead of 36^)
3. The ratio between the height of the upper part of the torso to that of the lower part in the case of a normal male figure is 0.66, where as the corresponding ratio in dwarf figure is only 0.48. What it means is that the upper part of the torso in dwarfs is relatively much shorter as compared to the lower part of the torso. This could be due to deformity or a hunchback.

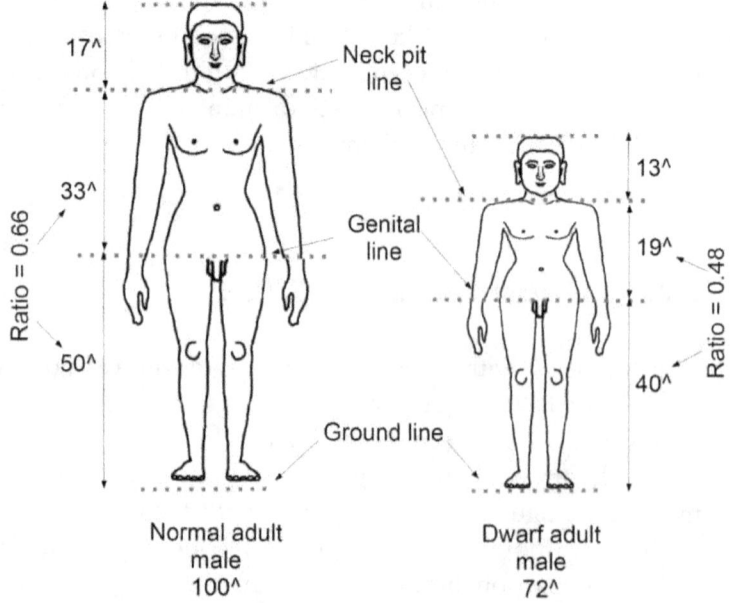

*Figure 4.1 Comparison between normal and dwarf adult human figures*

# Carving dwarf Gods

The Hindu mythology talks about a large pantheon of Gods each with a unique appearance and capability. The Silpa Sästra groups these Gods into various categories depending on their appearance and importance. Many of the major Gods fall in category 10. However, some Gods with distinct appearance fall in much later category. The most popular among these Gods are the elephant headed Ganesa and the monkey featured Hanuman. Interestingly both these Gods are considered to be dwarf. Accordingly, the Silpa Sästra puts them in the same category, namely the upper category 5. The total height of a figure in upper category 5 is 64 angula (i.e. 5X12+4).

Since Ganesa happens to be the most interesting and popular God, the Silpa Sästra gives special treatment to this God and gives detailed body measurements. I have summarized these measurements in Figure 4.2.

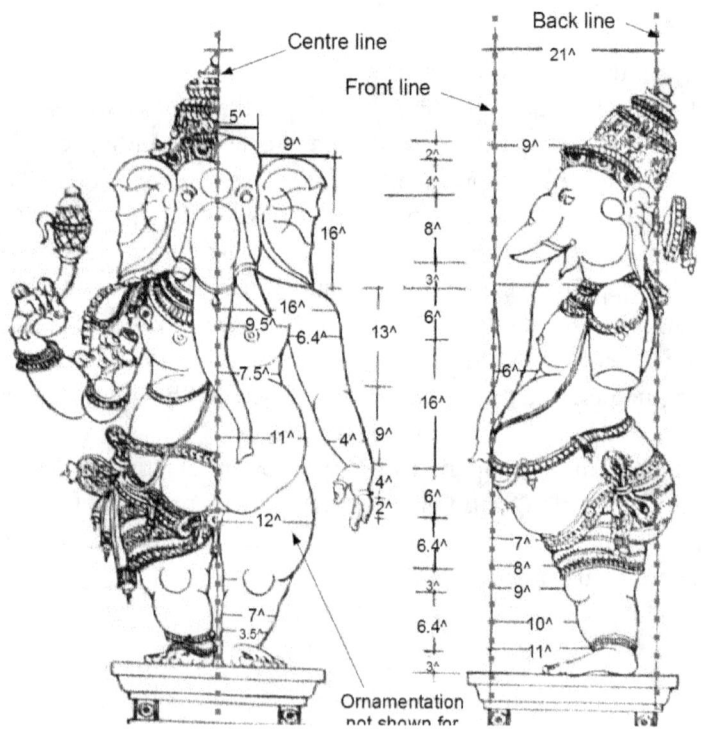

*Figure 4.2 Detailed measurements for Ganesa (Image adapted from Sri Kasyapa Silpa Sāstram by Jnyānānada)*

# Carving kids

The Kasyapa Silpa Sästra puts kids into category 4. It does not specify the age range of the kids. Some Silpa Sästras put the kids into category 3 into which tiny beings called Kinnars are also put.

Figure 4.3 is drawn based on the description of kid body measurements given in the Sästra. The figure also compares a kid figure with that of an adult figure.

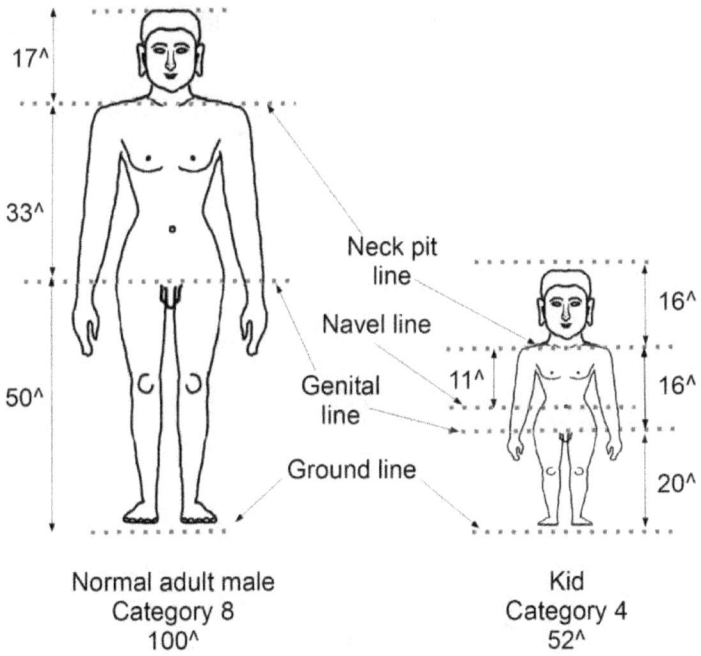

*Figure 4.3 Comparison between normal adult human figure and that of kids*

Following differences between adult figures and that of kids can be noted.

1.  The height of adult figure is 100 angula where as that of a kid is only 52 angula.
2.  The size of a kid's face is bigger relative to its body.
3.  While the centre of the body in adult figures is at the genital start point, that of a kid is higher up and close to its navel.
4.  Kid figures have relatively short legs.

In the last chapters we saw how the Silpa Sästra lists out body measurements of various figures. But body measurements are not everything. What else does a carver need to know while carving these figures? That is what we will discuss in the next chapter.

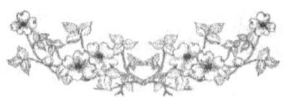

# 5. Just the body measurements are not all

**In** the previous chapters, we saw how these Silpa Sästras try to standardize various figures in terms of precise body measurements. But body measurements are only a small part of the entire thing. The Silpa Sästras also describe the way a figure appears – how it stands or sits, how many hands or heads it has, what weapons are held in each hand, the details of ornaments adorning its body, and so on.

These descriptions are mostly given in what are called *Dhyäna Shloka* (meditative verses) or *Moorty Laksana* (distinctive characteristics of the figure) for the figure. A Dhyäna Shloka or Moorty Laksana normally describes most features of a deity to which a figure corresponds. A person is supposed to meditate on that form of the deity to achieve a specific result. These verses also provide the basis for the sculptor to carve the figure accordingly.

A figure could be in a standing position (*Sthänu*), or in a seated posture (*Aseena*) or in a lying down posture (*Sayana*) or even in a dancing posture (*Nrtta*). Among these, figures in the dancing posture are the most intriguing.

The verses (i.e. Moorty Laksana) describing these postures can be quite elaborate and they spell out each and every detail of the figure. For example, the description of one of the most popular dancing posture of God Siva (shown in Figure 5.1) runs something like this

---

"... *the centre line for this figure should pass through the centre of the head (Ushneesa), centre of the forehead (lalata), end of the right eye (netranta), one angula right of the nostril (putanta), right of the chin (hanu), centre of the neck pit (hikka), centre of the navel (nabhi), centre of the left thigh (ooru), and the centre of the foot (päda) that is touching the ground....*

*.... the hand (upper left) holding the fire should be raised as much as to be in line with the neck pit line.... The hand (upper right) holding the mini drum (damaru) should be stretched as much as 28 to 40 angula from the front line (poorva sutra).... the lower right hand should display the abhaya mudra. The distance between the centre of this hand and the front line (poorva sutra) is approximately 24 angulas.... the distance between the heel of the raised left leg and the ankle joint of the stationary right leg should be around 45 angulas.... (Kasyapa Silpa Sästra Chapter 68)*

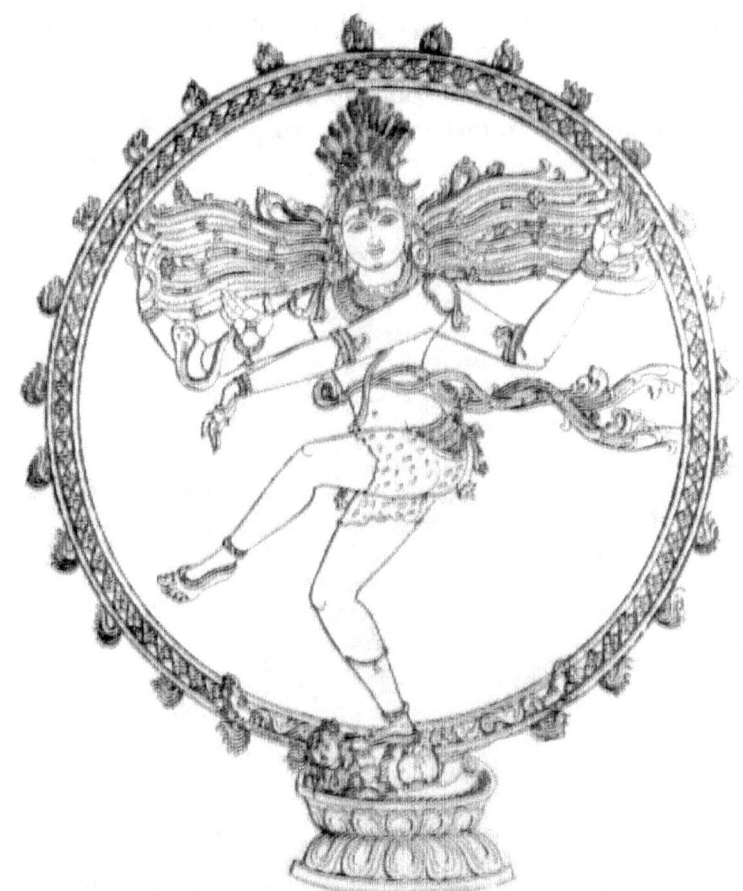

*Figure 5.1 God (Siva) performing a happy dance (Image adapted from Sri Ka-syapa Silpa Sástram by Jnyänänada)*

This is a posture where the God in the form of Siva dances blissfully (and hence the name Änanda Tän̲d̲ava). This is a four handed figure with fire in the upper left hand, a small drum called *d̲amaru* in the upper right hand, and the lower right hand gesturing the *abhaya mudra* (it means "fear not, I will protect you"). While the right leg is firmly pressed on the ground or placed on the Apasmära (an evil force), the left leg is raised in a dancing posture.

There are as many as 9 different dance poses described by the Kasyapa Silpa Sästra. Figure 5.2 shows one more of these interesting dancing poses. This pose is depicted with eight hands. The figure below the left foot is called *Apasmära* – probably indicating evil forces that the God crushes under his feet to protect his devotees.

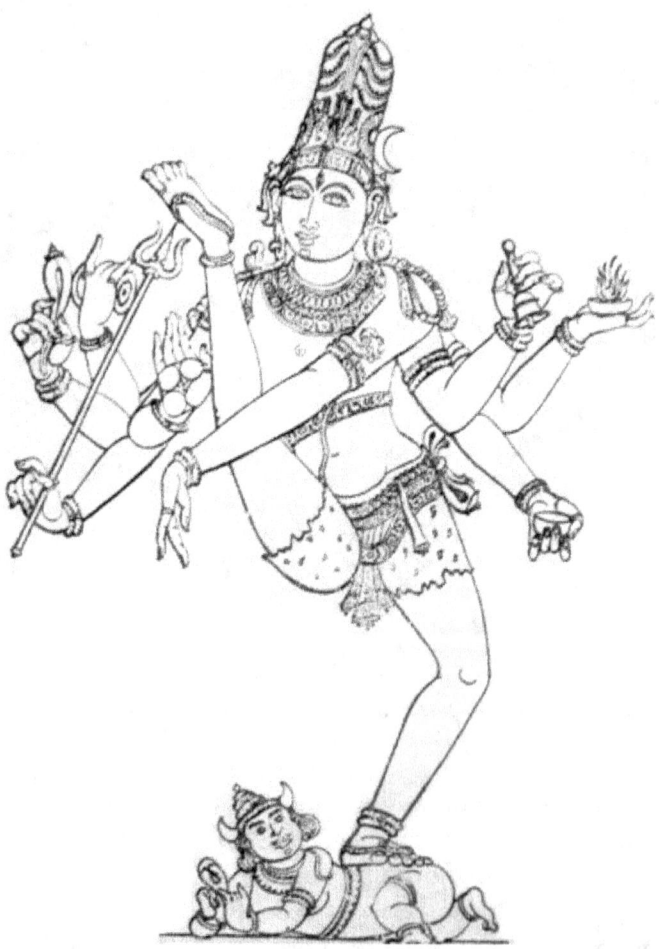

*Figure 5.2 One more dancing posture (Image adapted from Sri Kasyapa Silpa Sästram by Jnyänänada)*

Often the figures are not carved in isolation nor may they be meant specifically for the purpose of worship. They could form part of a scene that depicts a specific event or a story. These events are generally based on mythologies that are woven around the main character in the scene. So the carving could be more than a mere figure but a pictorial depiction of an entire story.

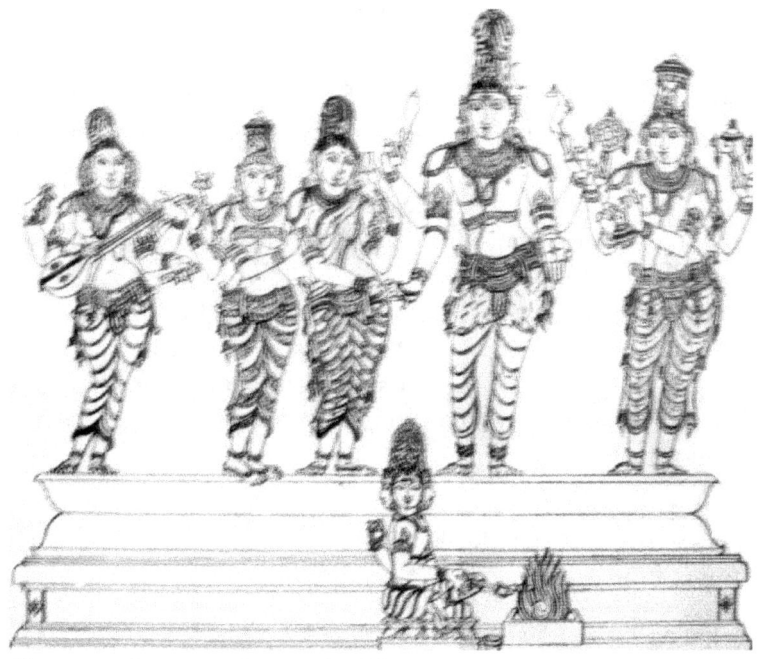

*Figure 5.3 Siva getting married to Narayani (Image adapted from Sri Kasyapa Silpa Sāstram by Jnyānānada)*

Figure 5.3 shows one such composition of several figures to depict the divine marriage of Siva with Nārayani. Brahma, Vishnu and Siva are the three Hindu trinities. In this composition, Siva is shown being married to Nārayani, the sister of Vishnu in the traditional Hindu style of marriage ceremony.

Vishnu is shown on the right (rightmost figure) of Siva – the bridegroom, and Vishnus's wife Laxmi is shown on the left (second from left) of Nārayani – the bride. Saraswati – the wife of Brahma is bearing witness to the ceremony and standing on the extreme left. The depiction shows the Pänigrahana (holding of hands) ritual as part of the ceremony. The four headed Brahma is performing the fire ritual as part of the ceremony (bottom seated figure).

There are many more such compositions we will be seeing in the next chapter.

Having covered measurements of various figures, descriptions of appearance of these figures, the composition of several images in a scene etc. in this and previous chapters, let me next show you some of the marvelous ancient figures that are carved based on the Silpa Sästra at various regions in and around today's India.

Many of these figures are those of Gods or mythological characters, and they do give an idea of the range of figures the Sästra tries to cover. You can also see the underlying similarity across distant regions even though there are minor regional variations.

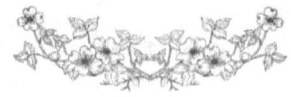

# 6. Some of the marvellous ancient sculptures

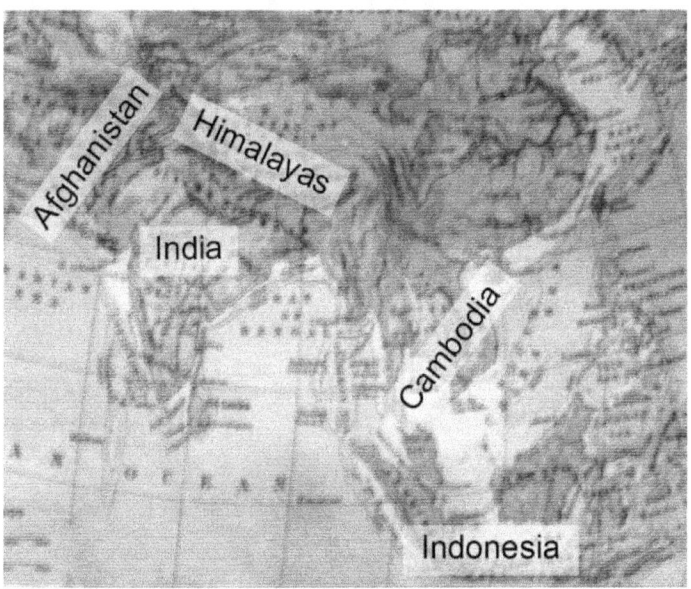

There is amazing similarity between ancient figure carvings found in a geographically wide area ranging from Afghanistan in the Northwest, to Cambodia in the extreme Southeast; from Himalayas in the North, to Indonesia in the far South.

*Figure 6.1 The Indian subcontinent*

This similarity is not merely due to the figures being human like in appearance, but also due to almost similar cultural and religious past shared by these regions. Similar kind of beliefs, mythologies, and art forms existed in these regions for centuries. The sculptures that we see today in these regions bear testimony to this fact. Though there may be regional variations in exact depictions, the overall theme is the same, as we will see later in this chapter.

Unfortunately, today many of these marvelous sculptures are either in ruins or in mutilated forms in many places, owing either to ravages of time or in some cases due to waves of religious intolerance that swept through this region at different times. The most recent case is the destruction of the renowned Bamiyan Buddha statues in Afghanistan by the Taliban extremists. The silver line is that this tradition of carving is almost well preserved in today's India, especially in the south, thanks to meticulously followed carving rules laid down in the Silpa Sästras.

Let me now show some of the interesting ancient sculptures that are more or less well preserved even to this day in this region. I will focus more on the images, little bit of its mythological background, and history of the carving where available. I neither intend to cover all images or regions in this vast land, but will present only some representative images. I will start with the interesting sculpture I saw in the carvers' village that I visited (recall Chapter 1).

# Dwarf with a lamp on his head

When I visited the carvers' village, one figure that fascinated me was the figure of a dwarf holding a lamp on his head. This is a bronze sculpture that I found in the village temple. You probably noted that I have used this image on the book cover. I reproduce it here for clarity.

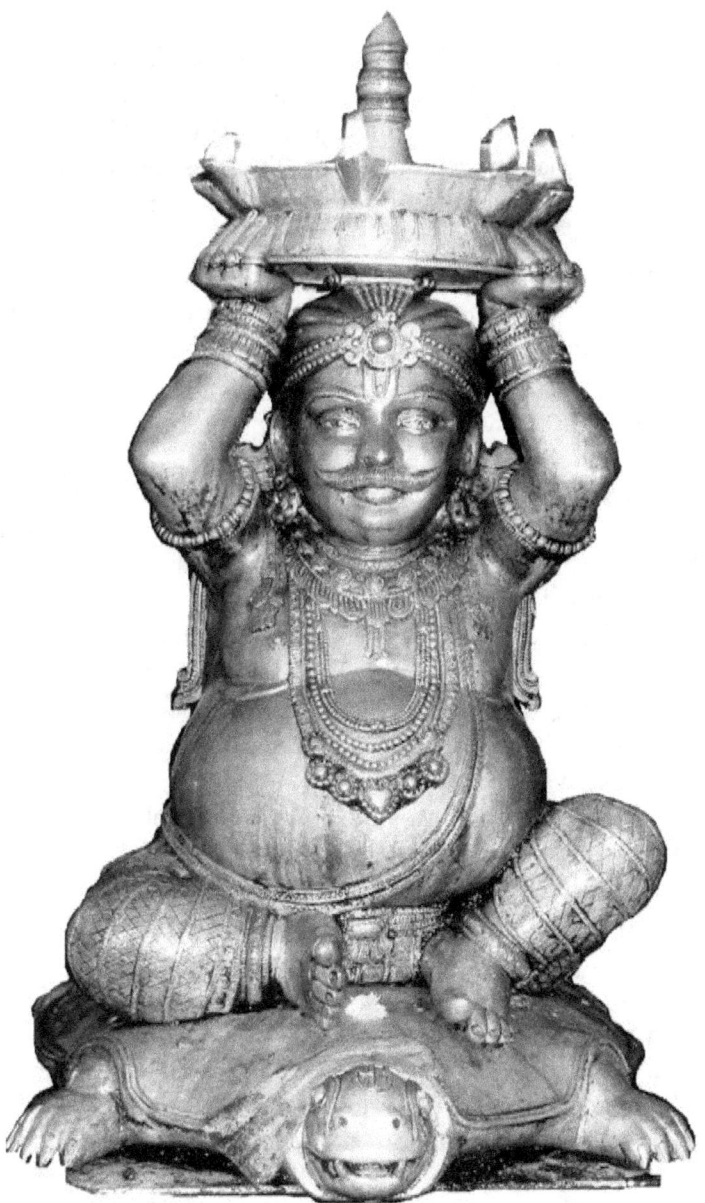

*Figure 6.2 A bronze figure used as a lamp*

This beautiful life size sculpture is actually a lamp with the dwarf's belly serving as a store for the oil that feeds the wicks burning atop the head of the dwarf. A clever design indeed!

I am not sure whether it is some ancient sculpture or a replica. But it surely provides an interesting model. A closer inspection indicates that it is sculpted as per the rules laid down in the Silpa Sästra. The figure seems to fit in category 5 to which dwarf Gods belong. It is quite an informative exercise to check the measurements by back calculation, if you wish.

Next let me describe another figure that always intrigued me for various reasons. It is the figure of Bähubali.

## Bähubali – the naked saint

This figure has always fascinated me for more than one reason. Firstly, it is probably one of the tallest intact ancient monoliths in the world. Secondly, the nudity is not meant to convey erotism but to put forth lofty ideals and as a symbol of renunciation. Thirdly, as we already discussed in Chapter 3, it is beyond imagination how such a colossal figure (almost 70 ft tall, weighing 2600 tons!) was carved, transported and erected in place, centuries ago when no cranes, motor vehicles or other modern gadgets were available.

It is the figure of King Bähubali who once ruled a kingdom in ancient India. His story goes something like this. Two princes Bharata and Bähubali fought over the kingdom. The younger of the two namely Bähubali won the fight. Instead of rejoicing his victory, Bähubali saw futility in going after worldly possessions. He renounced the kingdom that he has won and went to forest in search of everlasting peace. He meditated for years in a standing posture after donating whatever he had to the needy, including his dress to a beggar who had no clothes to wear.

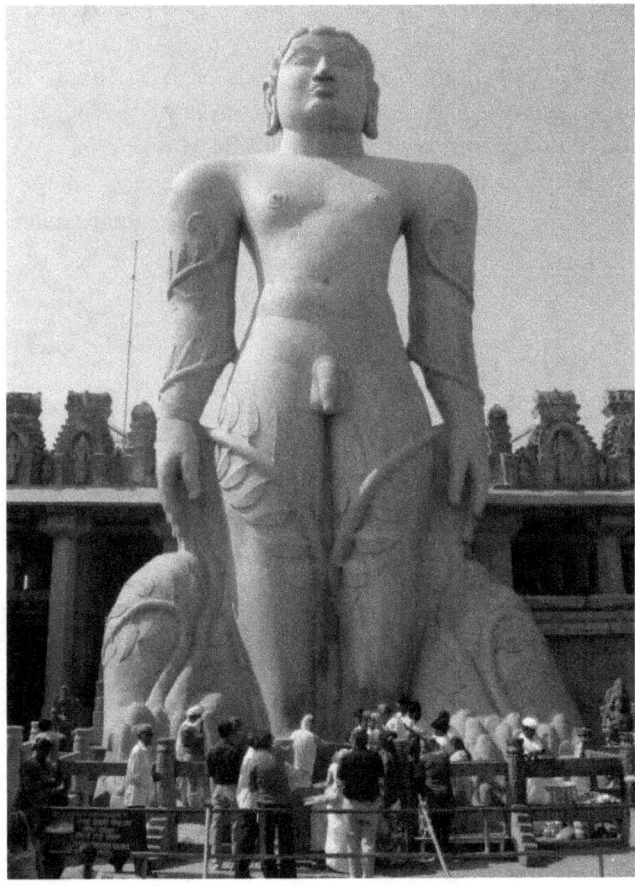

*Figure 6.3 Bahubali - the naked saint.*

Over a period of time wild creepers grew around his body and anthills surrounded him. But Bāhubali continued till he attained the ultimate realization bearing all the hardships. People were so impressed by his severe penance that they worshipped him as a great saint. His idols were later erected in the same naked standing posture in which he meditated.

## Brahma, Maheswara and Vishnu, - The Hindu trinity

The Hindu mythology has three Gods each in charge of creation, maintenance and final re-absorption of this world. They are Brahma – the creator, Vishnu – the sustainer, and Maheswara – the God in charge of final re-absorption of the world before the next cycle of creation starts. The high relief panel shown in Figure 6.4 depicts these three Gods.

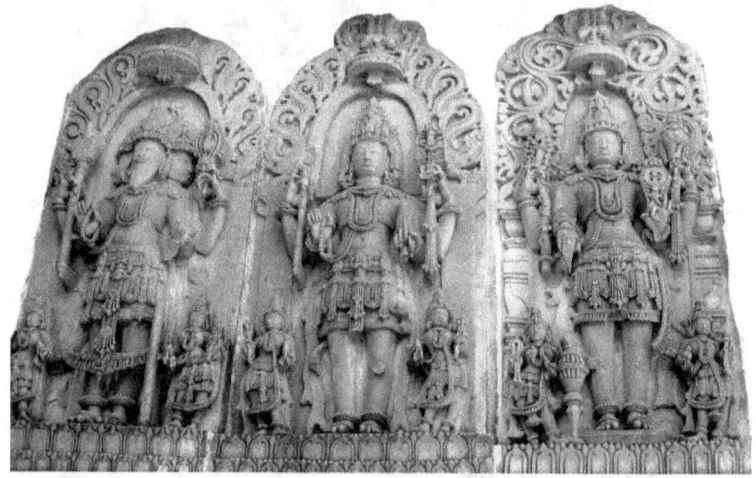

*Figure 6.4 The Hindu trinity*

Brahma – the first figure - is the four headed form of God who created this world. The four Vedas, the most ancient of Indian scriptures, are supposed to have been recited from each of these faces. One of his faces is bearded to indicate that he is the grandsire of all beings. He has four hands with weapons in his two hands. The other two hands hold a string of counting beads and a book (probably broken off in the figure). These are supposed to depict him as a source of all knowledge.

The central figure is that of Maheswara. Maheswara is the form of God that ultimately destroys this world at the end of the creation destruction cycle. He has one head. He has four hands. One of his hands holds the trident (broken off in the figure) and another, a special drum called *damaru*. Hindus believe that all vowels and consonants in any language are born from the sounds generated by this damaru.

The right most figure is that of Vishnu – the form of God that looks after the world. He has one head and four hands. The hands hold (from top left in clockwise order) a lotus (*padma*), conch (*sankha*), disc shaped weapon (*cakra*) and a club shaped weapon (*gadha*) which is broken off in the figure. The ornamentation in all these three figures is especially noteworthy.

What I showed in Figure 6.4 is Indian version of the Hindu trinity. The same Gods are depicted in a slightly different way in other regions of Indian subcontinent. For example, Figure 6.5 shows Java version of Brahma and Maheswara, two of the trinities.

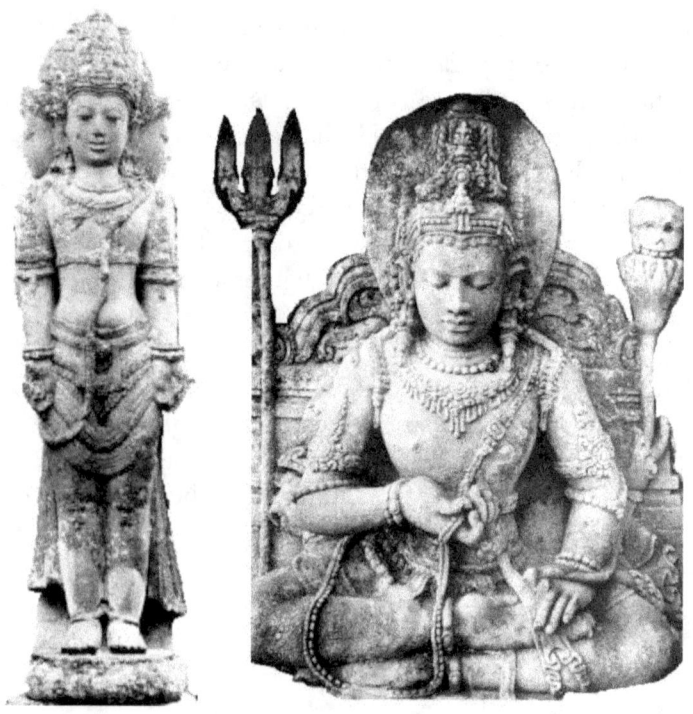

*Figure 6.5 Java version of Brahma and Maheswara*

The Brahma figure on the left has four heads just like its Indian counterpart. But it has only two hands and no weapons in these hands. The figure of Maheswara on the right has very little similarity with its Indian counterpart except for the trident which is a distinctive character of Maheswara figures. Even this figure has only two hands. Both figures are excellently decked with ornaments.

The Hindu mythology is replete with stories of clash between evil forces and divine forces. Every now and then an evil force surfaces and creates havoc in the world. The benevolent God takes myriad forms to slay this evil force and rescue the world. One such story is that of God slaying the demon who was in the form of an elephant.

## Gajasura samhara – Slaying of the Elephant shaped demon

A demon called Gajasura (gaja – elephant, asura = demon) – a demon in the shape of an elephant - was creating havoc in the worlds. The God took a fierce form with 16 hands each holding a lethal weapon and finally slayed the demon. The sculpture in Figure 6.6 shows this fierce form of God dancing on the head of the elephant shaped demon after killing him.

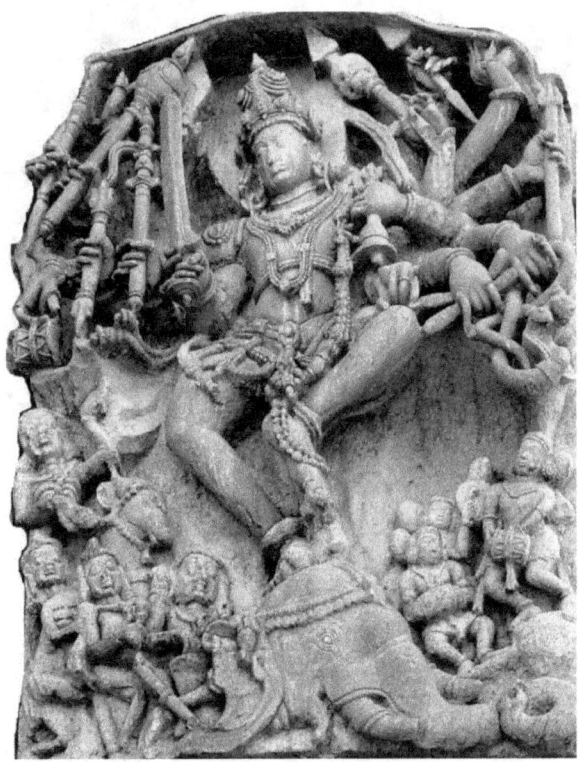

*Figure 6.6 Slaying of the Elephant demon*

Sometimes a demon can appear in other strange forms. In the

next figure, I will take up the slaying of a demon that is in the form of a buffalo.

## Durga – the slayer of buffalo shaped demon namely Mahisha

Viewing the God as a mother was quite prevalent in most parts of the ancient Indian subcontinent. Lot of mythological stories are woven around the female form of God. One of the most popular among them is that of Durga.

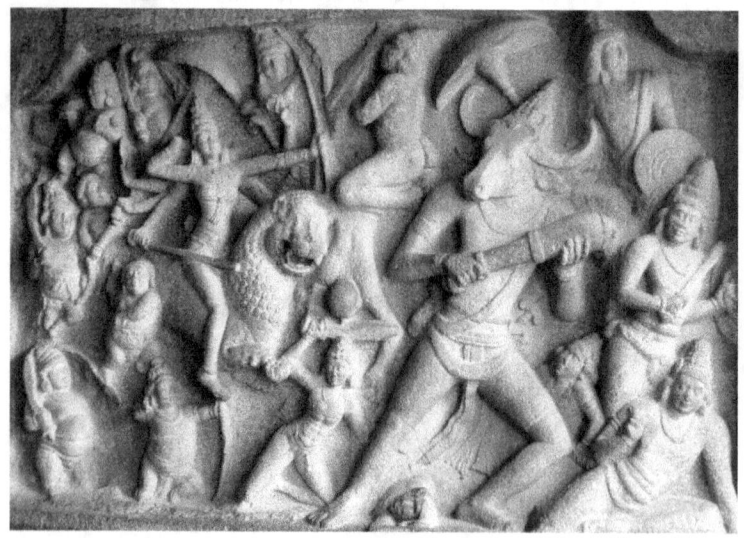

*Figure 6.7 Durga killing the Buffalo demon*

The story is something like this. A fierce demon Mahishasura (*Mahisha* = buffalo, *asura* = demon) in the form of a buffalo was running havoc in the worlds. He could not be killed by any man since he had received such a boon from God himself. Finally, the God had to take the form of an 8 armed female, riding a lion, to put an end to the havoc created by Mahisha.

What is shown in Figure 6.7 is a relief carving of the Indian version of Durga. Here the demon is depicted as half human half buffalo. Durga is shown shooting an arrow at Mahisha.

The same Durga with slight modifications is depicted in Figure 6.8. This is a Nepali (a Himalayan country) version of the same God, probably a three dimensional figure used for worship.

Observe the face of the Goddess which has more Nepali features. Also, she has many more hands than the Indian version. She is slaying the demon Mahisha lying at her feet with a trident and appears as if it is just a play for her. If you view closely you can see the beheaded buffalo from which the demon is emerging out in human form.

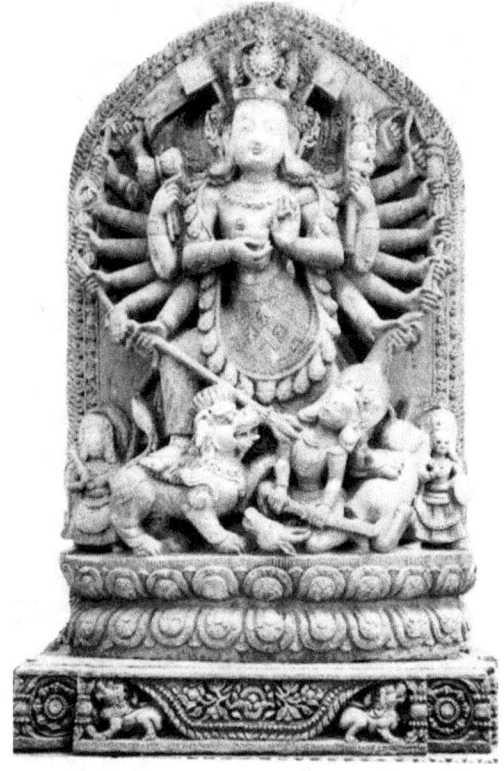

*Figure 6.8 Nepali version of Durga*

The same Durga takes on a slightly different form when she is depicted in far south namely in Indonesia. Figure 6.9 shows this Indonesian version where the buffalo is more evident.

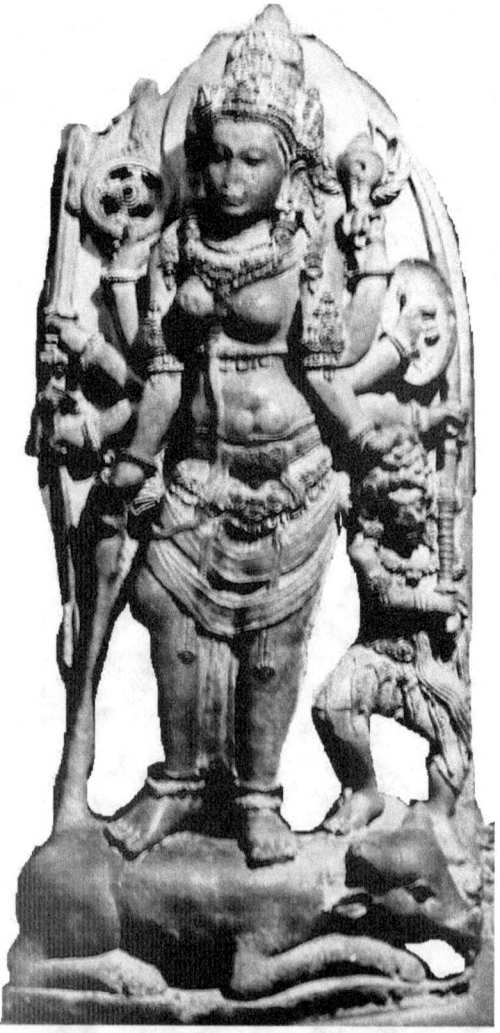

*Figure 6.9 Indonesian version of Durga*

In Indian mythology it is not just the evil forces that take strange forms, even the Gods take on such forms. One such interesting form which is quite popular in the Indian subcontinent is that of Narasimha.

## Half human half lion Narasimha

A cruel demon by name Hiranya Kashyapa pleased the God and got a tricky boon from him. As per the boon he cannot be killed by neither a man (nor God in human form) nor any animal; neither on the earth nor in the skies; neither during daytime nor at night; nor using any weapon whatsoever.

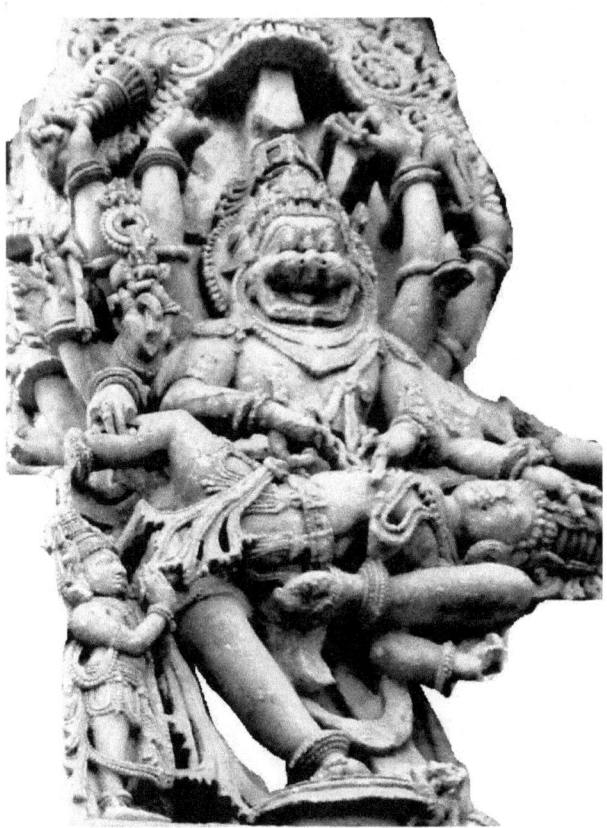

*Figure 6.10 Narasimha killing demon Hiranyakashapa*

After receiving this boon the demon was convinced that God

can never kill him and became very arrogant. He started creating havoc in the worlds. His son Prahlad who was a great devotee of God was the most tortured by this arrogant demon. The demon started denying the very existence of God and challenged his son to show the God to him.

Finally, the God had to appear one evening (neither day nor night) in the form of half man half lion (neither man nor animal), lift him onto his lap (neither earth nor the skies), and tear open Hiranya Kashyapa's intestines with his nails (not any weapon whatsoever) and kill him. Figure 6.10 depicts this fierce form taken by the God. You can see the young boy Prahlad standing obediently, in the bottom left corner. This is a typical Indian version of Narasimha (*nara* = man, *simha* = lion)

As always, same figure is depicted in slightly different form in other regions of the Indian subcontinent. For example Figure 6.11 shows the Nepali version of Narasimha killing Hiranya Kashyapa.

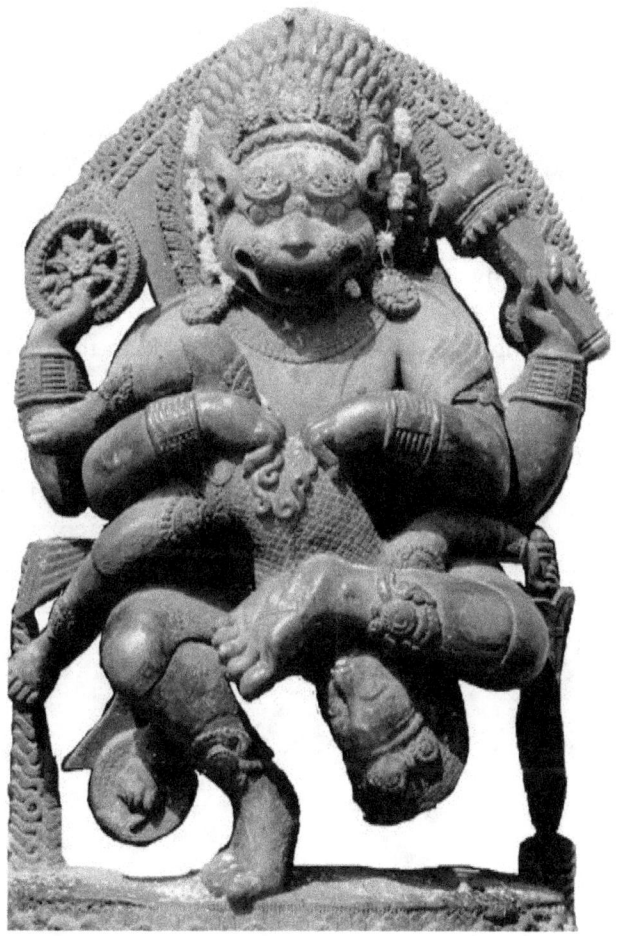

*Figure 6.11 Nepali version of Narasimha killing Hiranya Kashyapa*

One mythological story that finds mention not only in the Indian subcontinent but also in far off lands like Persia is the story of God taking the form of Trivikrama (one who has won the three worlds). Ancient Persian scriptures talk about this story. The story goes as follows.

## God covering the three worlds in three steps

A mighty king Bali who ruled over the earth once became very arrogant. He started to assume that he is the ruler of all the three worlds: heavens, earth and the nether worlds. God wanted to humble him.

So God came to him in the form of a small boy Vamana (literally means dwarf) and asked him for space measuring just three steps. Bali gladly promised the boy to satisfy his wish without realizing that the boy is none other than the God himself.

All of a sudden the boy Vamana grew into a giant spanning all the three worlds. He measured the skies with one step, and the earth with another. Bali realized his folly and offered his head to the God so that God can place his third step. This way, the arrogant King was humbled.

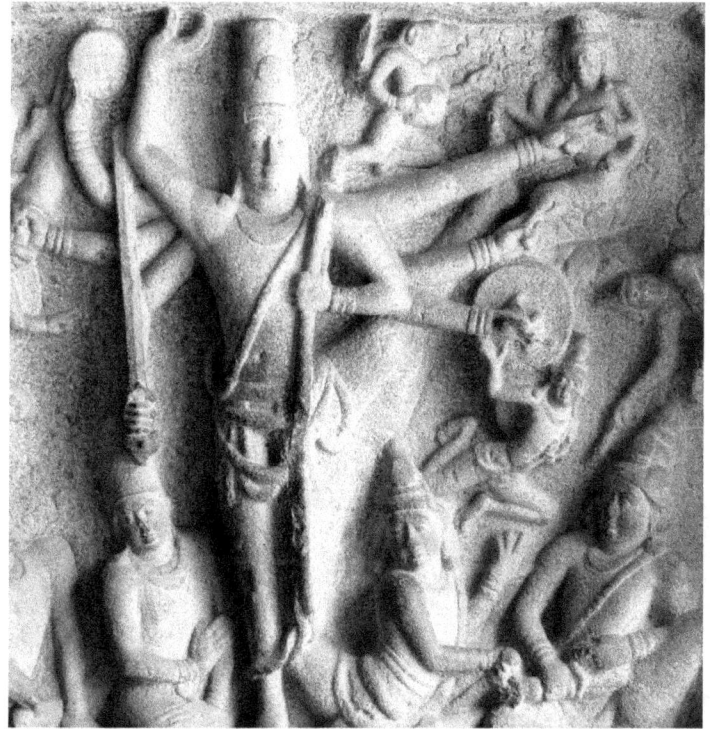

*Figure 6.12 Story of God turning from Vamana into Trivikrama*

Figure 6.12 depicts this story of Trivikrama in the form of a relief carving.

The great Indian epic Ramayana was so popular in the entire Indian subcontinent that the scenes from this epic often formed the subject for several carvings. I will just show two interesting examples.

## Ravana lifting the Mount Kailas

The ten headed demon king Ravana once wanted the God to come and reside in his palace so that his mother could worship the God every day. But the great God in the form of Siva residing in Mount Kailas refused to come to Ravana's palace.

Furious Ravana tried to lift and carry the entire mountain

along with the Siva sitting on top, with him to his palace. But unfortunately, he failed to do that however much he tried. He had to finally give up.

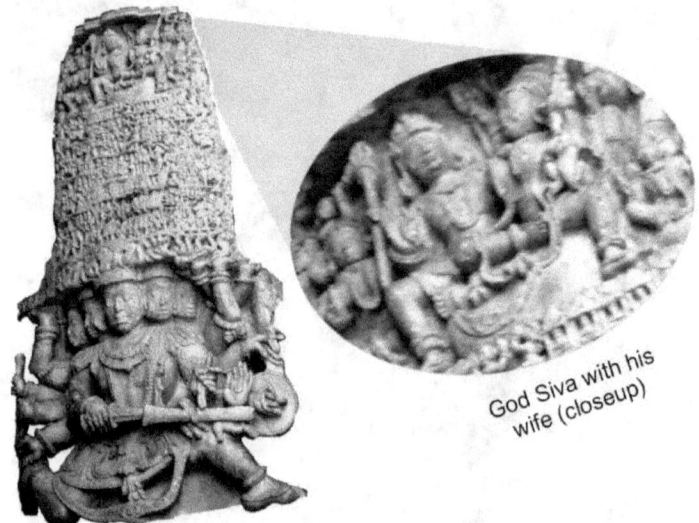

God Siva with his wife (closeup)

*Figure 6.13 Ten headed Ravana lifting mount Kailas*

This is quite an intricately carved piece which is unfortunately damaged to some extent. The details of the heavenly beings that reside in the mount Kailas are not clearly visible in this small picture. I have just given the close up of God sitting atop the mountain in Figure 6.13.

Another important event in the epic Ramayana is that of Ravana kidnapping Rama's wife Sita and carrying her to his place Lanka.

## Ravana kidnapping Sita

The ten headed demon king Ravana wanted to avenge the insult suffered by his sister from Rama. So he kidnapped Rama's wife Sita and carried her to his palace in Lanka, in a bird shaped airplane (called *pushpaka vimana*).

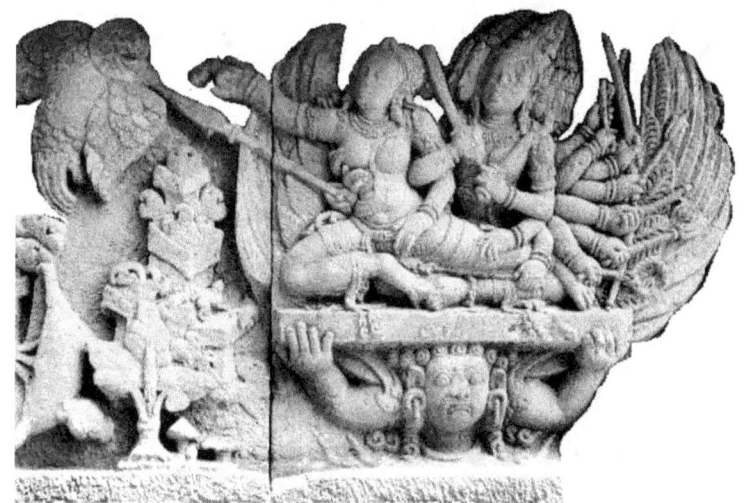

*Figure 6.14 Ravana kidnapping Rama's wife Sita*

On the way, Sita shouted for help. A giant bird Jatayu who was flying by, tried to stop Ravana from flying further. But the demon attacked Jatayu with his spear. Figure 6.14 shows an Indonesian version of this episode in the form of a relief carving. Look at the depiction of the airplane with two wings on both sides, and a demon supporting it on his head. The bird Jatayu is on the extreme top left corner.

It is not just the Hindu images that are found in these regions. This region went through a time when Buddhism was quite popular. Whether it is in extreme left borders of Afghanistan, or the south east borders of Cambodia, or even in its southernmost border of Indonesia, Buddhist sculptures could be seen. Unfortunately these sculptures are in ruins today due to religious intolerance and many of them can be found only in museums.

## Buddhist images

Figure 6.15 shows a beautifully carved image of meditating

Buddha, much larger than life size. Look at the calm serene face of this Indian version of Buddha

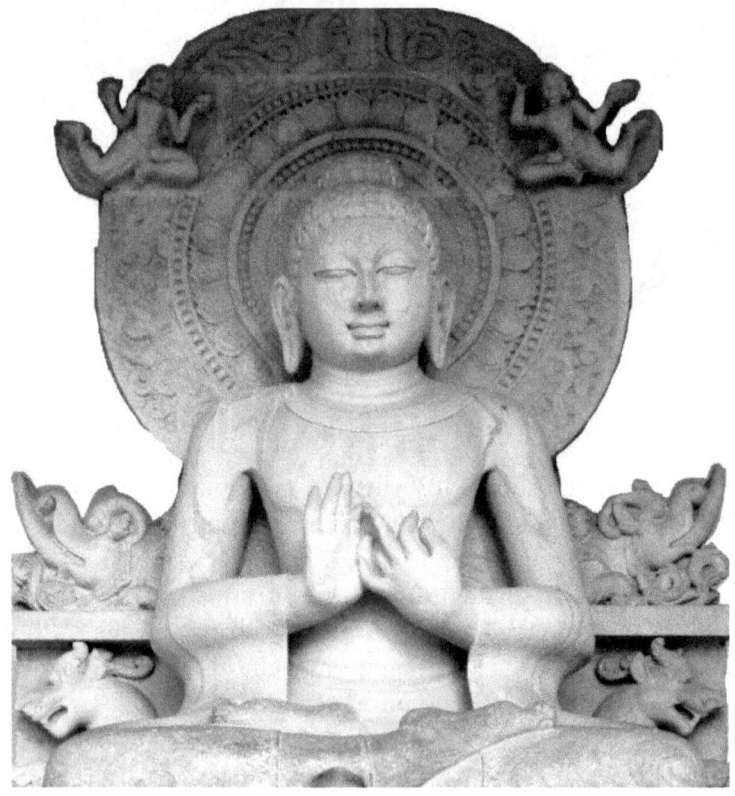

*Figure 6.15 Meditating Buddha*

Similar serene faces can be seen in other regions as well. Figure 6.16 shows the bust of a Buddha statue from Afghanistan.

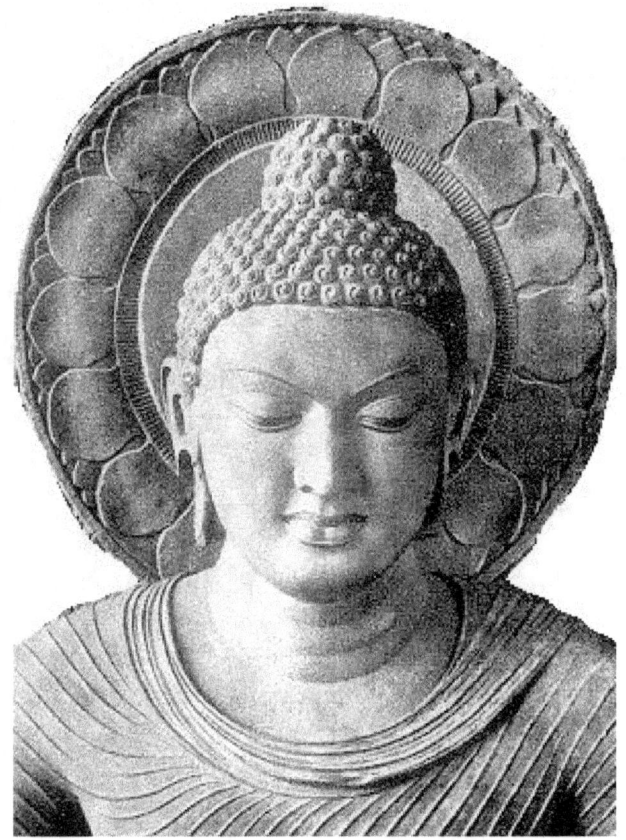

*Figure 6.16 Afghan version of Buddha*

Though we normally see Buddha in a meditating pose, there are many relief carvings narrating incidents from the life of Buddha. For example, Figure 6.17 shows Buddha comforting poor and helpless people.

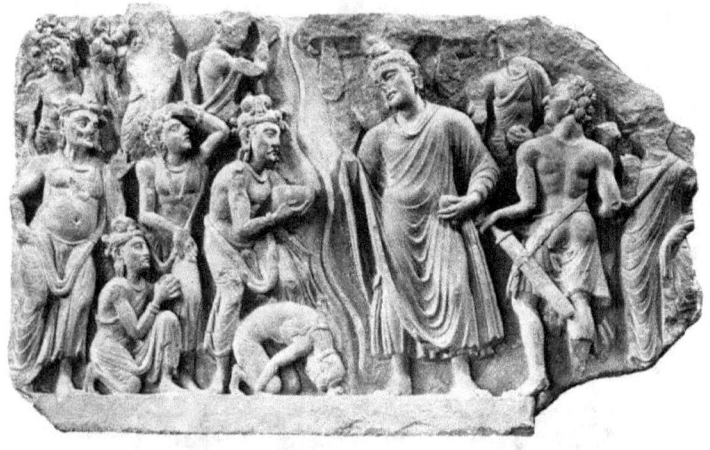

*Figure 6.17 Buddha comforting poor helpless people*

The variety of sculptures that are found in this vast region (i.e. the Indian subcontinent) is so diverse that not just the religious figures but also figures depicting ordinary events are also elaborately carved. Let me show two simple relief carvings depicting a hunting expedition, one from Cambodia and another from Indonesia.

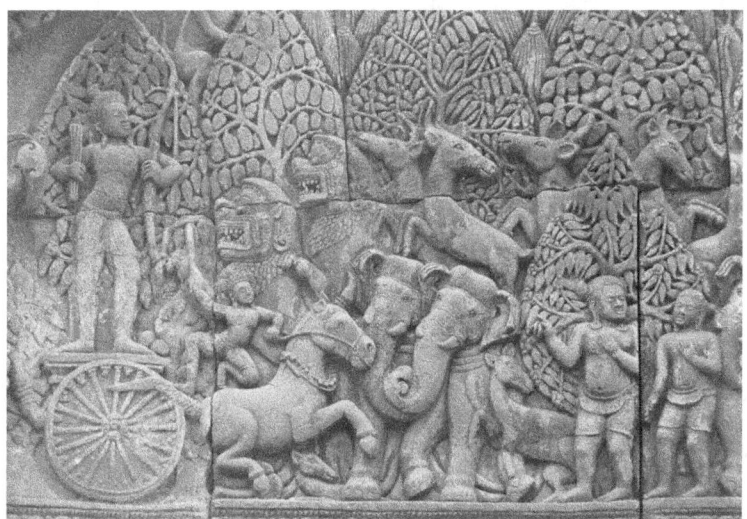

*Figure 6.18 Cambodian version of a hunting scene*

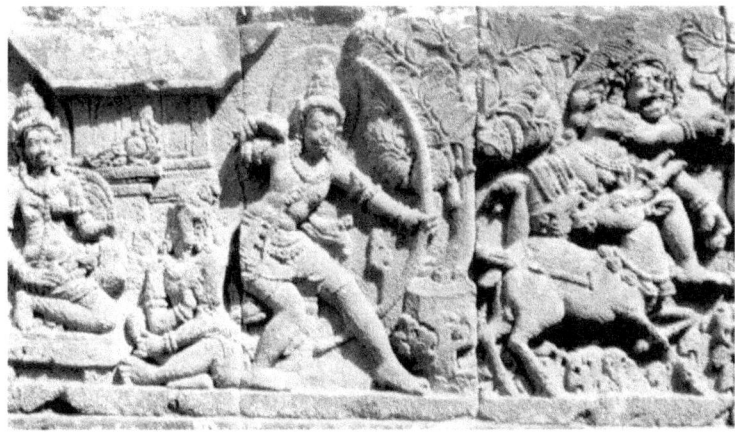

*Figure 6.19 Indonesian version of a hunting scene*

In yet another display of day to day events of common man, the intricately carved Cambodian piece shown in Figure 6.20 depicts two men fighting over the possession of a woman, while many onlookers eagerly watch the drama.

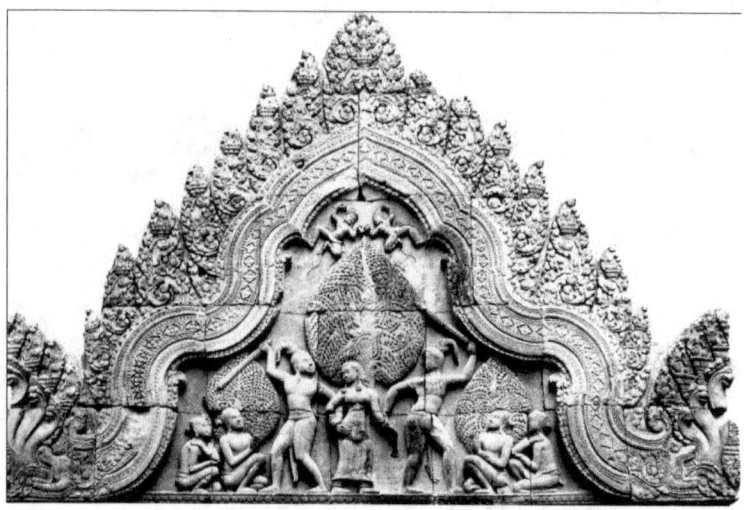

*Figure 6.20 Two men fighting for a woman*

Having covered all aspects of life - religious, social and so on, the sculptures found in these regions don't lag behind in depicting erotic sculptures as well. In fact there are many temples in these regions that stylistically depict romantic poses. But what makes it intriguing are tens of temples that exclusively depict various erotic poses. These are the temples found in one place namely Khajurao in India.

## Erotic sculptures of Khajurao

Erotic sculptures are not uncommon in ancient Indian temples. But none can be as explicit as those found in a series of temples in Khajurao.

Nudity was never a taboo in ancient Indian mythological depictions. In fact, the Silpa Sästras give detailed measurements of each part of the human body including the genitals, breast etc. But temples exclusively dedicated for showcasing sex in all forms is something puzzling.

Various explanations are given, but probably the main source of inspiration could be the well known treatise *Vatsyayana Kamasutra*. This is a treatise exclusively on various aspects of sex.

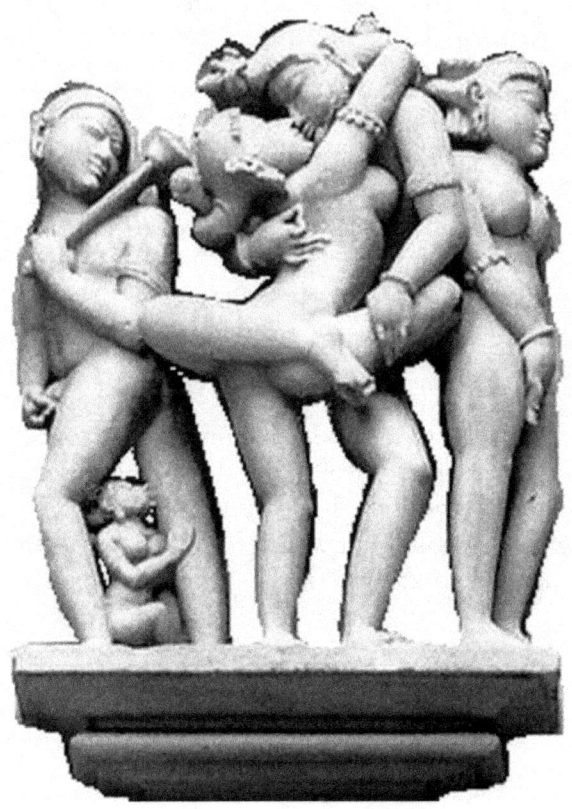

*Figure 6.21 One of the many erotic sculptures found in Khajurao*

There are many many more interesting sculptures in these regions. But I will stop at this.

# How about creating some of your own?

If you seriously want to try out some of these figures, or create figures of similar style, you probably need the original images that you can enlarge or resize to your need. I can provide the images as a zipped file so that you can use them for that purpose. But let me remind you that many of these images are copyright protected and it will not be possible for me to make them available publicly.

However, for your personal use, I can provide them with a caution. Please request through my blog **http://doctor-king-online.blogspot.com**, by posting a comment on the "ask me" page on the right. Don't forget to indicate your <u>e-mail address</u> to which I have to send the file, and also let me know <u>where you bought the book from</u>.

Your comment will not be made public, nor your e-mail address, which will be used solely for this purpose. Please do try to write a review about the book on the seller page from where you bought the book. That will not only be useful for me but also to other carving enthusiasts. I will greatly appreciate that.

I conclude this book with some interesting observations in the next chapter.

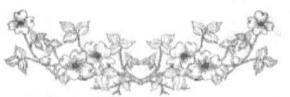

# 7. Some interesting observations

**Whatever** I discuss in this chapter may not strictly come under the purview of the subject matter of this book. However, I feel that these observations help in clearing some misconceptions often harbored by some people both within and outside the Indian subcontinent.

The ancient religions like Judaism, Christianity or even Islam, all have monotheism as their core belief. These religions also stress on formlessness of the God though he is assumed to have human like qualities – love, affection, anger, mercy and so on. After seeing a series of images of Gods in the previous chapter, it is tempting to jump to the conclusion that the ancient religion in these areas was that of idolaters who believed in polytheism. To some extent this conclusion was responsible for the religious intolerance and consequent destruction of several ancient figures in these regions.

What I want to highlight in this chapter is that the concepts of monotheism, formlessness of the God etc. are not unique to Judaism, Christianity or Islam. Even the ancient people in these regions held these views. The most ancient literature of these regions namely the Vedas held the view that a single God is called by different names.

> *"They refer to as Indra, Varuna, and so on. But the fact is that the same one is called by different names by the clergy".(Rig-Veda Book I, Section 164, Verse 46)*

Throughout the Upanishads (the philosophic parts of the Vedas), the uniqueness of God is stressed. God is assumed to be the creator as well as the nourisher of the universe.

> *In the beginning this (Universe) was nothing but the Ätma (i.e. God). There was nothing else at that time. The Ätma thought - 'let me create the worlds'. (Aitharëya Upanishad 1.1)*

The Vedas not only declare that the God is formless, but they go a step further and say that the God is indescribable.

> *"That which cannot be described by words, but that from which words get revealed, know that alone as the God. And not that worshipped by people as an object.*
>
> *That which cannot be comprehended by the mind, but that by which the mind works, know that alone as the God. And not that worshipped by people as an object.*
>
> *That which cannot be seen by the eyes, but that which is the force behind the eyes, know that alone as the God. And not that worshipped by people as an object.*
>
> *The eyes cannot see that, words cannot describe that, and mind cannot comprehend that. We actually have no way of instructing that."*

> *(Këna Upanishad 1.5-1.8, 1.3)*

In fact, the Vedas interchangeably use the pronouns *He/ She/ It/ That* when they refer to God to further stress the point that the God has no specific gender or form.

Having said this, one may wonder why idol worship was so

prevalent in these regions. The Bhagavad Geetha, another ancient Indian scripture gives the following reason.

> *For people who are conscious of their bodies (i.e. dominated by the body), it is difficult to meditate on a formless God (Bhagavad Geetha 12.5)*

The Bhagavad Geetha further says

> *"Compelled by their innate nature, ignorant people worship different deities by following various rituals in order to attain different desires.*
>
> *God bestows on such people the faith in such deities if they so wish.*
>
> *If they worship those deities with complete faith, those deities would give them whatever they desire, as decided by the God.*
>
> *But the results of such worship are only short lived.*
>
> *The foolish people assume that the God has different forms, but in reality the God has no specific form."*
>
> *(Bhagavad Geetha 7.20-7.24)*

Does it sound like a contradiction of ideas? Well, I would like to see it more as a balancing act between philosophic truths and practical difficulties of mortals with limited wisdom, as the priest who recites the following mantra while installing the God's image in a temple says.

> *I welcome you, Oh God of all Gods, who is the creator of the worlds, who is the father of all beings, who pervades the entire universe.*

*As an ordinary mortal with limited wisdom, I have created this form for my convenience in worshiping you. Please have mercy and make your presence felt in this image. (God installation mantra in Kashyapa Silpa Sästra)*

There is a difference between worshipping an idol as God, and using the idol as a medium to perceive God. I feel that what the ancient people in these regions actually did was the latter, while being conscious of their limitations and the ultimate truths.

Setting aside all these tricky issues, I would like to view these images as marvelous examples of celebrating human form in various ways. This surely gives unlimited scope for a serious figure carver to expand the horizons.

Welcome to a new world of figure carving. Enjoy carving!

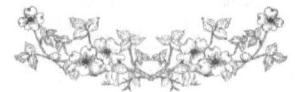

# Bibliography

1. *Kashyapa Silpa Sästra,* Original Sanskrit composition by Maharshi Kashyapa.

2. *Sakalädhikära,* Original Sanskrit composition by Maharshi Agastya

3. *Sarasvatiya citrakarma Sästra* Another original Sanskrit composition.

4. *Sri Kashyapa Silpa Sästram* by G. Jnyanananda, Karnataka SilpaKala Academy.

**Thank** you for reading my book. I hope you enjoyed reading it. Please give me your feedback through book reviews. I appreciate that very much. You may contact me through my blog at http://doctor-king-online.blogspot.com I will be happy to hear from you. If you have any specific questions or suggestions, indicate them through my blog and I will surely respond to them.

You may also be interested in reading my other books available through several online vendors.

# My recent books

Following is the list of my recent books. These are available both as e-books as well as paperbacks. Some of these books are now available from one or more of online bookstores such as

Amazon, Scribd, Smashwords, Apple iBookstores, Barnes & Noble, Sony, Kobo, Flipkart Diesel eBook Store, eBooks Eros, Baker & Taylor, Page Foundry ,WH Smith in the UK, FNAC in France and Portugul, Livraria Cultura in Brazil, Angus & Robertson in Australia, Bookworld in Australia, Indigo in Canada, Collins in Australia, Feltrinelli in Italy, Libris in the Netherlands, Paper Plus in New Zealand, Play in Great Britain, Rakuten in Japan, Rakuten in the US, Whitcoulls in New Zealand.

Please look for them in your favorite book store. You can always use the book title in your search to see if the book is available in your favorite bookstore. I have given the appropriate links for your convenience in my blog http://doctor-king-online.blogspot.com

## 1. Figure Carving – The Ethnic Style : *Amazing world of possibilities*

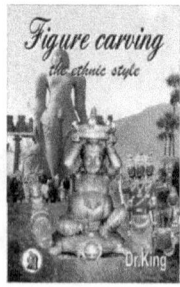

Book synopsis:This book opens up a new world of figure carving options for carving enthusiasts. It provides an unlimited number of options not only in style but also in technique backed by detailed illustrations and lots and lots of carving pictures. Add an altogether new dimension to your carving repertoire.

## 2. Five simple Grafting techniques best suited for most exotic fruit plants

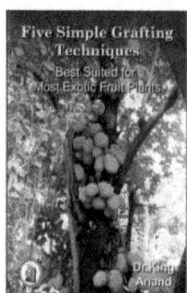

Book synopsis: This book describes in detail 5 most useful grafting techniques that can be used to propagate many exotic fruits. The book contains detailed illustrations, examples, fruit chart as well as root stocks and techniques well suited for these fruits.

### 3. How does the Mind work?

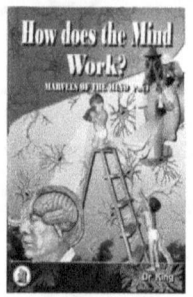

Book synopsis: This book explains the highly specialized subject of working of the mind in an easy to follow style using day-to-day examples. It gives latest information based on current research, focusing on key contributions.

Apart from providing the readers with the latest scientific information about the functioning of the mind, the book lays the foundation for the discussion in later parts of this series about the working of Yoga and Meditation.

The book adopts a structured approach allowing the reader to pick and choose not only the area but also depth of coverage depending on individual interests.

## 4. Important missing dimensions in our current understanding of the Mind

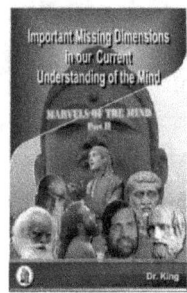

Book synopsis: Our current scientific achievements in understanding the working of the mind are commendable. However, in it's over insistence on objectivity science seems to have overlooked some important dimensions of the mind. There are many questions science fails to provide satisfactory answer.

Interestingly, many of these questions were addressed by ancient philosophies and probably in the true scientific spirit we should look at these philosophies with an open mind.

This book focuses on these missed dimensions and how ancient philosophies address them. A range of ancient philosophies, amazingly well conceptualized, that look at different aspects of the mind are discussed in the current book.

There is the ancient philosophy of Plato who points out the limitations of our sense perception, the elaborate psychology of ancient Buddhists that almost parallels with our scientific understanding, the philosophy of Śankara who even questions the reality of existence and the concept of domains beyond mind that are the focus of ancient Upanishads. All these, and more, are explained clearly in this second part of the series.

These philosophies compel us to rethink on our current definition of science and its approach. The book also provides a smooth transition point from science to philosophy and finally to domains beyond both these.

## 5. How and Why of Yoga and Meditation: *Yoga scientifically explained*

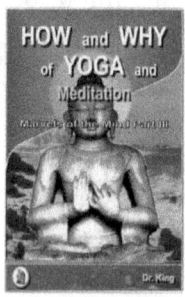

Book synopsis: This book gives a clear insight into various aspects of Yoga, while providing scientifically backed explanation about how various Yoga processes achieve their intended purposes and why they are designed that way. Such clarity is essential to understand Yoga in a more scientific manner and to realize its full potential.

The book also explains in a step by step manner how various processes of Yoga, namely the body postures, breathing techniques and meditation are performed and why each of these processes is needed to attain complete benefit of Yoga.

This book is a good guide for anyone who wants to practice Yoga.

## 6. Yöga Facts: *Answers to some important questions about Yöga*

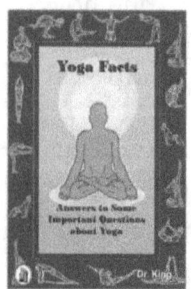

Book synopsis: Going by the large number of books on Yoga that are published and sold both through printed as well as electronic media, this ancient science seems to be very popular. While various things are propagated in the name of Yoga, there is often mismatch between expectations and achievements.

This short set of questions and answers clears some of the misconceptions about Yoga by drawing attention to the original works on Yoga dating back more than 2000 years. Questions that often arise as a result of commercially motivated propaganda are answered in a matter of fact manner. At the same time, this book reassures a sincere Yoga practitioner, that the goal is not only achievable but worth the effort.

Some of the questions discussed include - controversies due to adverse scientific findings about Yoga, why many people fail to achieve any progress in spite of sincere efforts, and so on.

## 7. Psychology behind Yoga: *Lesser known insights into the ancient science of Yoga*

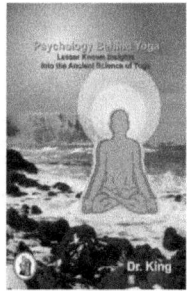

Book synopsis: Though Yöga is well known as a process to achieve the ultimate realization, not much attention is paid to its psychological underpinnings. This book builds up the theory behind Yoga based on descriptions given in ancient texts such as Yoga sutra of Patanjali (~200 B.C.) and Sänkhya Kärika of Īšvara Krishna (~300 A.D.). This understanding is essential to get a complete grasp of the Yöga process.

This book clearly explains the concept of mind as defined in Yoga Sutra and Sänkhya Kärika, various states this mind can be in, and how by a step by step process the mind can be nudged into the ultimate desirable state namely the Samadhi. It discusses various hindrances one encounters while going through this process as well as how these can be overcome. As often mistaken, samädhi is not a single state but a series of progressive states one goes through as one progresses into the Yoga practice. This book explains those stages both with reference to the original sources as well as through simple analogies.

The ultimate state of Yoga, namely the niruddha state of mind is also very well explained, its implications and what exactly happens in that stage.

## 8. Ancient wisdom – Modern viewpoints: *Interesting picks from ancient Indian scriptures*

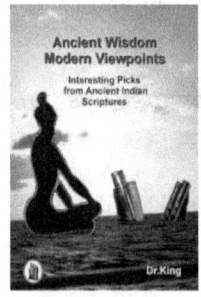

**Book synopsis:** This book captures the essence of ancient Indian scriptures, analyzing them from today's point of view. The scriptures selected are mainly the eleven Upanishads (parts of Vedic literature), Bhagavad Geetha (most important book of Indian philosophy) and the Manu Smrthi (one of the most ancient law books by Manu). All these scriptures were composed more than 2500 years ago and influence the Indian way of life even to this day. In addition to these primary scriptures, this book also cross references several other ancient Indian scriptures such as Yoga Sutra of Patanjali, Sänkhya Kärika, Närada Bhakti sutra, and Dammapada.

Some of the key aspects of each of these three main scriptures – Upanishads, Bhagavad Geetha and Manu Smrthi - are picked and presented in 6 short, crisp articles. While writing these articles, the original Sanskrit texts are relied upon with minimal re-interpretation.

Adequate references to the original Sanskrit verses are given in most places, to impart authenticity to the rendering. To help the readers who may not be familiar with Sanskrit, simple English translations of these verses are also provided.

This is an ideal book for anyone who wants to have a quick overview of most of the ancient Indian scriptures. The book gives a wealth of information and surely a key to the treasure of ancient Indian scriptures.

## 9. A Mantra to enhance your mental capabilities

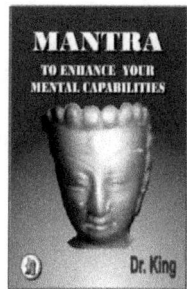

Book synopsis: For thousands of years, millions of people have taken advantage of one mantra which is believed to enhance the mental capabilities. Though it is used even today, it has become a prerogative of a small minority of people and seems to be going into the oblivion. The ravages of time has seriously rendered this potent mantra into an article of religious faith and deep rooted superstition, depriving the vast majority from realizing its benefits.

This book opens up this mantra to all those who are desirous of enhancing their mental capabilities. It discusses various aspects of this mantra and explains in a step by step fashion how anyone can take advantage of this mantra.

## 10. Around the Mind

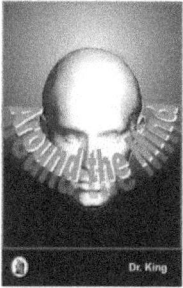

Book synopsis: Mind may probably be the most intriguing thing that has fascinated human beings, philosophers as well as the scientists, for thousands of years.

This book summarizes our current scientific views on the Mind, the questions that arise due to that view, the efforts by ancient philosophies to address these questions and probably a possibility of going beyond the realms of current scientific approach.

It also introduces Yoga as a way to go beyond the realms of mind.

www.ingramcontent.com/pod-product-compliance
Lightning Source LLC
Chambersburg PA
CBHW072028190526
45166CB00015B/972

* 9 7 8 1 5 1 9 5 0 2 0 8 7 *